Doing The Impossible

THE 25 LAWS FOR DOING THE IMPOSSIBLE

Patrick Bet-David

Valuetainment Publishing

Doing the Impossible

Copyright © 2011 by

Patrick Bet David

All rights reserved.

Originally Published July 2012

Updated Edition November 2016

Published in the United States by

Valuetainment Publishing

ISBN-13: 978-0-9976223-0-0

REVIEWS AND QUOTATIONS:

Individual excerpts of 50 words or less for inclusion in commercial book reviews is permissible.

Quotes by current or historical public figures and the descriptions of their lives was taken from multiple public reference sources assumed to be credible. These sources were researched and vetted as much as was reasonably possible. The author and publisher do not make any absolute claim as to their accuracy.

Learn more information at: www.PatrickBetDavid.com

Other Books by Patrick Bet-David

The Life of An Entrepreneur in 90 Pages

The Next Perfect Storm

More books coming soon. To see all books by Patrick Bet-David, visit his Amazon Author Page.

Acknowledgements

Let me start off by acknowledging how fortunate I am to have met my wife Jennifer, who is the best thing that ever happened to me. It takes a very special woman to marry a man like me, and God hand-selected her to be right next to me as we go on this journey called Life. I thank God every day for giving me a wife like her - she is also an absolutely amazing mom to our 3 children.

I want to thank my parents Diana and Gabreal, who had the courage to escape our war-stricken environment in Iran and bring us to the land of all opportunities. It was an interesting journey of getting here but it was all worth it. It's a responsibility of mine to represent my bloodline in a way that makes both of them proud.

If there's a man I can call my hero it would be Gabreal Bet-David. It's a rare thing nowadays to have a father who isn't concerned about pleasing you all the time because he knows that he's responsible for raising a man who can stand on his own. My father has done exactly that. Anyone who has ever met my dad will tell you that spending an hour with him isn't enough. You want him around all the time. His wisdom is priceless.

I have to thank two of the greatest listeners in the world who are willing to sit there and listen to me as I bounce ideas off of them for hours. I rarely get any response from them, but just the fact that they listen makes a world of difference. The names of those two individuals are Jimbo and Kucci, my two little Shih Tzu dogs. I'm sure they will be thrilled as they read this acknowledgment of their efforts over the years.

I would like to thank Annie Freshwater for employing her strongly trained editor's eye. I also want to thank Chris Perez for keeping things organized and moving this project along.

A special thanks to Thomas Ellsworth, who joined me at PHP in 2015, who gives me the peace of knowing that if every single dictionary, encyclopedia, and the internet were to cease to exist, I would still have a source to go to who has all the answers. Your mind is faster than a Mac computer, Tom.

I'd like to thank many of my friends all over the country who took the time to read the manuscript while it was going through its different stages of development. Your honest feedback was invaluable.

Last but not least, I'd like to thank all of those who have challenged and inspired me over the years in all areas of my life (this is quite a list!):

Kim Sinclair, my health and guidance teacher in high school, who inspired me to join the Army. Drill Sergeant Green, who pushed me to a limit I had never been pushed to before in boot camp. All of my Army buddies from the 326ENG Battalion in Fort Campbell; I would need a whole book to share the stories we experienced together. Bradford, Guttierez, Aghakianest, and McLroy, who were all crazy in their own way and helped make the experience extremely entertaining.

Francisco Davis, who was the best sales manager in the world and who believed in me when I didn't believe in myself. Dave Kirby, who gave me the opportunity to start my career in the financial industry at twenty-one years old at Morgan Stanley without having the required college degree. Mauricio Terrazas, who introduced me to a division of Aegon where I had the opportunity to travel all over the world and work alongside many gifted and talented individuals as well as meet my wonderful wife.

Bill Vogel, who invited me to a special event in March 2009 where George Will was the key note speaker and inspired the Saving America Crusade.

My sister Polet Bet-David, whom I love dearly; I learn every day from the example she sets of what an incredible mother she is to my two little best friends, Grace and Sean. My brother-in-law, Siamak Sabetimani, who I believe is a saint.

To all the PHP leaders who decided to embark on the great awakening of Saving America at a time when all the odds were against us. I admire your excellence in building, your unity, your courage, and your touch of madness with a spoonful of competition and a sprinkle of craziness. You inspire me more than words can describe.

Bob Hastings, Richard Kennedy, and Lance Wilson, who inspired me to start a radio show on KKLA called "Saving America."

Pastor Dudley Rutherford, who constantly was in my ear while I was making some of the most important decisions of my life.

I especially want to thank our competitors and critics who remind me on a daily basis that I'm still alive; the day they stop, life stops. Thank you for your efforts.

Let's go make history.

Table of Contents

Introduction

GROWING UP AS A KID in Iran, I remember admiring different heroes like He-Man, Alexander the Great, Muhammad Ali, and Rocky Balboa. I clearly remember watching Rocky IV over and over again with tears in my eyes as "The Italian Stallion" did the impossible and beat the huge Russian boxer "Drago." As I watched the movie, I envisioned myself being the hero. Even as a seven-year-old kid I wanted to feel what Rocky was feeling right in his moment of triumph.

Do you remember those days? Do you remember dreaming about being a champion, making a difference, making history? Don't we all dream about making our family proud? To some extent, we all want to be heroes. We have a desire to deliver for our loved ones, the ones who count on us, to earn their love and respect.

Hollywood makes money by creating movies to make you believe for a split second that you can be Rocky, Rudy, Patton, or Alexander the Great. The downside is that a person spends $20 to watch that hero instead of being that hero himself.

In order to do the impossible, you have to tap into what motivates you. It all starts with the dream. If you don't have a vision that drives you to do the impossible, the mechanics of how to get there are irrelevant. This book is meant for the person who envisions a life of greatness. That vision looks different to each person. Greatness can be seen in the athlete who always gets the ball with three seconds left to make the winning shot; his team knows that his focus, talent, and drive will put the ball in the basket. Greatness is seen in the Navy Seal team that enters an enemy compound with years of preparation and training, showing extraordinary courage in the face of extreme danger. But greatness is also found in a single mother who works all day, takes care of her children, and still finds the dedication and perseverance to start a business and change her family's life. The principles that lead us to achieve the impossible can be applied to any goal. No matter what your dream looks like, you must first have the vision of where you want to go and what you want to achieve.

Do you remember as a child how we believed that anything was possible? When people asked us what we wanted to be someday, we answered with things like an astronaut, the President of the United States, a football star, or a famous singer. Do you ever ask yourself how we lost that imagination that we used every day as children? The same gift of imagination that allows a child to turn pillows and blankets into a fort is the power that we as adults need to tap into to imagine ourselves as the people who we want to become. Children's imagination and vision are limitless because they have not yet repeatedly been told that their dreams are too difficult or unrealistic. A child doesn't worry about failure or disappointment. As adults, we too often let our doubts and fears keep us from attempting to reach our dreams.

This book is for those who have a desire to achieve greatness and are ready to take the steps to turn that desire into a reality. At one point or another in this book, you will experience several different reactions—excitement, curiosity, joy, laughter, or even tears—but the ultimate goal is to encourage and challenge you to make a decision to do the impossible. That may have a totally different meaning to you than it did to Steve Jobs, Thomas Edison, or any of the other role models we will look at; but whatever doing the impossible means to you, the goal of this book is to help you realize that you have the capacity to do what the critics think is impossible. You can become a hero.

So don't hold back your thoughts and ideas when you're reading. Make notes in the book if you need to. I have a tendency to write notes or ideas that come to my mind all over the books that I read. There will be many opportunities for you to do so. You're not in a classroom with rules to break. Here's your shot to do things your way. My main challenge to you is to make a decision to read this book in less than two weeks in order to have your mind be sharp as you are putting all of these ideas together.

Free Companion Workbook

To get the most out of this book be sure to complete the action steps listed.

For your convenience, we've created a free PDF workbook to accompany this book. You can get your free workbook here:

http://www.patrickbetdavid.com/dti-workbook/

Dare to Do the Impossible

MANY THINGS THAT WE TAKE for granted today were once considered impossible. Visionaries know that what can be imagined can be achieved. Although people cross the world today in giant jetliners, one hundred years ago the Wright brothers had to first believe that human flight was possible. On May 6, 1954, Roger Banister became the first man to run a mile in under four minutes. It had never been done before and was therefore considered physically impossible. But since 1954, many runners have accomplished the same feat. Roger Banister's legacy is that he had faith that this act was possible before anyone else dared to believe.

No one ever thought that Buster Douglas would beat Mike Tyson. The odds were 42:1.

Prior to the sixties, no one ever thought we would land on the moon.

Back when mail was delivered via the Pony Express, who could have imagined a machine that sends mail electronically in seconds?

What would this world be without washing machines, cars, cameras, the Internet, cell phones, planes, televisions, or computers?

Ask yourself this: What if Armageddon happened tomorrow and everything was disintegrated except for you and ten other people? There's nothing left. How would you build a washing machine? A car? A computer? How would you create the Internet? Do you ever pause to think about that? We don't consider what that really means, to build the Internet from scratch. It seemed impossible to most people until it was invented.

> *"If they can make penicillin out of moldy bread, they can sure make something out of you."*
>
> — *Muhammad Ali*

Now imagine that it is twenty years after Armageddon and you're trying to explain to all the young people what the world was like with cars and computers and all the things that they have never seen. Would they think you're crazy? What if they asked you to rebuild that lost technology? Rebuilding might take a long time, but at least you would get to start out knowing for sure that such technology is possible.

These are all things that we need to think about to understand that nothing in this world is impossible. The only limits are the ones that we place on ourselves. Whether it was the first automobile, the idea of electricity, or the moon landing, the believer who first imagined the impossible made it possible for others to believe it and achieve it.

If the impossible throughout history has become the imaginable, and then the actual, why do we think that our dreams are impossible for us to accomplish in our own lives? Are we afraid to try for fear of failure? Isn't refusing to try the only real guarantee of failure? Remember, you miss 100% of the shots that you don't take. The first step to achieving the impossible is having the courage to attempt it.

> "It's never too late to be what you might have been."
>
> — George Elliot

According to the dictionary, to dare is "to have the necessary courage or boldness for something; [to] be bold enough." Achieving the impossible is not for the timid. It is not the safe and secure road. It means taking a leap of faith, leaving your comfort zone, and risking failure for the chance of success. There will be failures on the road to greatness. Thomas Edison had thousands of failed attempts at the light bulb before inventing the one that worked. Roger Banister said his 4:03.6 mile in 1953 "made [him] realize that the four-minute mile was not out of reach." Part of daring to achieve the impossible is letting failure motivate you rather than discourage you.

Think about some of the greatest stories of triumph and courage. Why do we love movies like Braveheart, Rocky, Gladiator, and Miracle on Ice? Yes, they are all stories of achieving the impossible. But more importantly, we admire the courage and perseverance of heroes who have overcome tremendous challenges. We find inspiration in those who reach for the impossible, fight against overwhelming odds, and turn past failures into stepping stones on the path to success.

So before you read the rest of this book, ask yourself: Do you dare to do the impossible? Most people let the fear of failure or fear of the unknown keep them from making the decision to pursue their dreams. Fear is the most destructive emotion for personal transformation. Fear thrives on the unknown. Our imaginations run wild with possible negative scenarios. By choosing to put yourself in situations where you have to face your fear, you learn that it is far easier to face reality than the endless loop of possible challenges your mind creates. The feeling of overcoming fear in turn gives you confidence to face the next challenge.

> *"Our lives improve only when we take chances— and the first and most difficult risk we can take is to be honest with ourselves."*
>
> — *Walter Anderson*

Making the decision to pursue the impossible is scary at first. You will have to face your fears and throw away your excuses. Start out by believing two important things:

1. You are capable of greatness.

2. Facing your fears to realize your dreams will be the best decision you ever make.

Law 1: Invest In Your Identity

HAVE YOU EVER THOUGHT about your identity? Not just your name and vital statistics, but what and who you are? Where we are in life is based on our identity. Our beliefs are based on that identity. Our future worth and opportunities will also be based on our identity. Many people think that if they change their circumstances (e.g. get a new, higher paying job), their identity will follow suit. This approach is actually backwards: In reality, we change our identity from the inside out and the change in our circumstances follows.

Let me give you two scenarios to illustrate how your identity becomes your reality:

First we have John, who is used to making about $30,000 per year. In 2006 during the housing boom, John gets a job selling mortgages and does really well. John starts making $200,000 per year over night. The problem is that John still has a $30,000 identity. That is the way that he sees himself. So in order to make himself feel more like that $200,000 earner, John goes out and buys a new Porsche and Armani suites and takes an expensive vacation to Europe.

Fast forward two years. The housing bubble has popped, and John is back to making $30,000 a year. Worse yet, he spent rather than saved the extra money he was making during his boom time. In fact, John spent more than he earned and is now in debt from his attempt to look the part of success on the outside, rather than focusing on the inside.

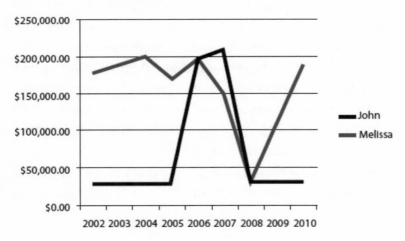

Melissa, on the other hand, is a business owner who is used to making over $200,000 a year through several

successful business ventures. Melissa's business gets hit hard by the recession, and in 2008 she only makes $30,000 in income.

If I were a betting man, I would bet money that within a short period of time Melissa will be back to making a high six-figure income. The reason why is because that income is her identity. That is how she sees herself; she believes she's worth $200,000 per year and she understands the principles needed to get there.

It's the same reason people who come into an inheritance or win the lottery are often broke again a few years later: They never built the identity of a successful high-earner. The running joke about the lottery is that it is a tax on people who are bad at math. People who think that buying lottery tickets is a wise use of their money are probably not going to be very good at managing their winnings on the 1 in 13,983,816 chance that they do win. To put those odds in perspective, if you bought one lottery ticket a week for 250,000 years, you would be expected to win once.

Consider the story of Jack Whittaker Jr. (1), a West Virginia businessman who became famous when he won $314.9 million in the Powerball multi-state lottery. At the time it was the largest non-divided jackpot in American history. Whittaker opted to take a lump- sum payment that came out to $93 million after taxes. Since winning the Powerball, Whittaker's life has gone dramatically downhill.

Since December 2002, Whittaker has:

- had two deaths in his family from drug overdoses,

- been sued by casinos for gambling debts,

- been sued by individuals looking for a payout,

- been robbed,

- been mobbed by requests for money every-where he goes,

- lost all of his friends,

- had his gambling, drinking, and philandering woes splashed about the media.

History and state lotteries have shown us that those who come into very large sums of money without earning it—or without having the identity to keep it—often end up broke again or worse off than they were before they won the money. Money is something that has to be grown into with a developed sense of discernment, responsibility, and wisdom.

As with anything else, before you begin to build your identity, you must first decide what you are building. Think about the college athlete who sees himself as one day being a professional basketball player. Once he gets drafted by the NBA, where else can that identity take him? He has already arrived. Now think about stars like Michael Jordan, Kobe Bryant, or Phil Jackson. Their identities are based not just on being in the pros, but on being one of the great ones of the game. They attract that level of success because they see themselves that way and therefore do the work to make it a reality. Sometimes it may take years for us to actually transform into the person we see ourselves as; but if we truly believe that is the person we are meant to be, eventually we find a way to embody that identity.

Building your identity is about earning that identity. It is about doing the hard work, seeking the information, and transforming yourself from the inside out into the person who you envision becoming. This book will hopefully give you the tools and Items to begin that transformation.

Winston Churchill gave a speech at Harvard University on September 6, 1943, which he closed by saying, "The empires of the future are empires of the mind." If you want your future to look different, you have to start by changing your thinking and building your identity into the person who you desire to be.

An associate of mine asked me a question once on why his identity wasn't constantly growing, so we did an inventory of the way he spent his hours each week. Here is what we found:

- 168 total hours per week

- Sleep: 7 hours per day x 7 days = 49 hours. (119 hours left)

- Work (including drive time and lunch breaks): 10 hours per day x 5 days = 50 hours. (69 hours left)

- Watch TV: 4 hours a day x 7 days a week = 28 hours. (41 hours left)

- Personal hygiene / bathroom / shower: 1 hour a day x 7 days = 7 hours. (34 hours left)

- Workout/exercise: 1.5 hours x 3 days = 4.5 hours. (29 hours left)

- Family responsibilities / church / soccer practice: 10–30 hours a week. (Time is gone)

The real question I asked was, "Out of your 168 hours per week, how many hours do you spend reading, listening to personal development CDs, attending professional development conferences, or associating yourself with high identity individuals?" His answer was an hour a week. I asked, "How do you expect an hour a week to compete with the other 167 hours?" If you want to transform your identity, you must make the process a priority in your life. The time that you spend on your identity makeover will positively transform all the other areas of your life as well.

Action Items

#1: How many hours a week do you spend working on your identity? _____

#2: What are three things you're willing to commit to in order to help increase your identity?

1. _____

2. _____

3. _____

Recommended Videos

10 Books for Entrepreneurs:

http://www.patrickbetdavid.com/top-10-books-for-entrepreneurs/

How to Change Your Reputation:

https://www.youtube.com/watch?v=CKD1624bIiw&t

Law 2: Let the Right Ones In

THERE'S AN ADAGE THAT SAYS that you will make the average income of the five friends with whom you spend the most time. For better or worse, we become more like the people who we hang around. Your associations have a lot to do with where you're at in every area of your life. The idea is to create an "advisory board" of friends who will lift you up, challenge you, inspire you, and hold you accountable. Your friends are going to influence you either way, so why not pick the friends who will be a positive influence?

Birds of a feather ...

1. Walt Disney befriended Ray Kroc while the two were working together as ambulance drivers back in 1917.

2. Bill Gates and Warren Buffett have become friends and partners in their philanthropy.

3. Magic Johnson and Larry Bird were both competitors and friends. They both spoke the same language of doing the impossible.

4. Two of the most influential American authors of all time, Ralph Waldo Emerson and Henry David Thoreau, lived in the same small town and were close friends. Their dialogue helped shape each other's philosophy.

5. Another famous friendship existed between writers C.S. Lewis and J.R.R. Tolkien. The two became the best of friends not just because of their shared belief in the power of myth and writing, but also because of shared religious beliefs.

Making the active decision to change your associations can lead to some painful criticism. For example, you realize that if you want to make it to the NBA you need to stop playing ball with your friends at the YMCA and instead start running with players at a much higher level. Your YMCA buddies who can't relate to your burning desire to go to the NBA may feel like you are leaving them behind, or they may think that you feel superior to them. Some friends may even try to bring you down out of envy of your courage and confidence. Some people simply have no desire to attempt the impossible in life. That's okay, too. We all get to make choices on how we want our life to be.

"Associate yourself with people of good quality if you esteem your reputation, for 'tis better to be alone than in bad company."

— George Washington

Very rarely will you have friends who will completely support you for what you're doing. My father once told me that finding a true best friend is just like finding a great spouse: One special person is worth more than hundreds of acquaintances. A true best friend will build you up and believe in you. Lesser friends, and even family members, may not. Sometimes they are worried that they are being left behind, or perhaps they simply lack your belief.

> *"People are like dirt. They can either nourish you and help you grow as a person or they can stunt your growth and make you wilt and die."*
>
> *— Plato*

Believe it or not, this is where most people hesitate when pursuing their dreams. They let the criticism and doubts of others get to them and they give up. Prepare yourself for criticism or lack of support from people around you and make the decision ahead of time not to let it deter you from your path. Any time you decide to make a courageous change in your life you will have naysayers, even some who are doing it out of love or concern for you. You can't control the criticism that you'll get, but you can control your reaction to it.

> *"Wounds from a friend are better than many kisses from an enemy."*
>
> — *Proverbs 27:6*

Think of your associations in terms of assets and liabilities. People who are assets are your mentors, your guides to an increased identity. Look for people who have qualities that you want to develop in your own self and learn from them—someone who holds a leadership role in life, for example, who has faith as a cornerstone, has been married for thirty years, and has raised good kids.

> *"First they ignore you, then they ridicule you, then they*
>
> *fight you, then you win."*
>
> — *Ghandi*

It's not a complex formula: Look for people who have the attributes that you want in your own life. Be selective of your friends. Think about the identity that you want to build for yourself and create associations in your life with people who resemble that identity. Last but not least, keep in mind that people want to associate themselves with others who add to their lives. If you constantly bring value to others, you will be someone who others seek to associate with as well.

"All truth passes through three stages. First it is ridiculed. Secondly, it is violently opposed. Third, it is accepted as being self-evident."

— *Arthur Schopenhauer, German Philosopher*

Action Items

#1: Study your associations. Make a list of the five friends with whom you spend the **most** time. Remember the key is the most time. How do they influence you in a positive or a negative way?

Name	Positive Influence	Negative Influence

#2: Your most important associations: finding true mentors

A true mentor is worth his or her weight in gold, but mentors are not easy to find. Think of a person in your life currently or in the past who you believe served as a mentor to you. Let's take a closer look at that person. There are some keys to look for when determining if someone is a true mentor.

Key qualities:

1. They care about you.

2. They're not afraid to give you tough love.

3. They challenge you regularly.

4. They teach you by setting a great example of success themselves.

5. They have a great vision.

6. They have a solid foundation of character—a good personal life as well as business life.

If you are lucky enough to have someone like this in your life, your job is to become very coachable. Be grateful for your mentor. A true mentor is a rare treasure. Earn your mentor's respect and show him or her that his or her belief in you was well-founded. That will be all the payment that a true mentor needs.

#2: Make a list of the associations that you would like to develop. What pastor, community leader, coach, or entrepreneur do you want to influence you? Then think about ways that you can develop your relation-ship with that person and spend more time with him or her.

Name:
How to develop relationship: _____   _____   _____

Name:
How to develop relationship: _____   _____   _____

Name:
How to develop relationship: _____   _____   _____

Name:
How to develop relationship: _____   _____   _____

Recommended Videos

17 Ways to Keep Talented Leaders in the Company:

http://www.patrickbetdavid.com/lose-talented-leaders/

How to Choose a Mentor:

http://www.patrickbetdavid.com/how-to-choose-a-mentor-seek-trifectas/

Law 3: Protect Your Credibility Score

ACCOMPLISHING THE IMPOSSIBLE requires you to earn the trust of others. You must prove to associates, friends, and family in your life that your word and your character can be counted upon. Trust takes years to develop but only moments to destroy. When the people in your life who you interact with know that you can be trusted, you will develop business and personal relationships that stand the test of time. Long-term, successful relationships are key to doing the impossible; nobody reaches greatness alone.

You need to be a person who people will want to work with long term. You have to be a bridge builder, not a bridge burner. There is no quicker way to burn bridges than by breaking the trust of those you have worked with. If you lack integrity in your dealings, it will soon be known by everyone. On the flip side, if you are a great partner, people will tell others and they will come back to work with you again and again.

"Nearly all men can stand adversity, but if you want to test a man's character, give him power."

— *Abraham Lincoln*

Even a person with the best intentions can fail in the credibility department. Sometimes it's a question of committing to too much, of not wanting to say no, or of not placing enough value on your word.

If there were a formula to run a "credit check" to determine what your FICO score is on keeping your word, how would you do? If you were to run my report in 1997 I would've probably scored around 400. That's because I had big dreams but very little action. I began working on my credibility FICO score as soon as I realized how powerful a person becomes when he strengthens his own word. It starts off with small promises you keep and leads to big commitments where someone will put a lot of trust in you because you have earned it. Do not make any commitments that you are not 100% sure that you can keep. Learn to say "no" or "let me get back to you." In the end, people will respect you more when your word is as good as gold—and you will respect yourself much more, too. You will eventually get to the point where you and all those around you know that if you say you're going to do something, it will get done.

"There are seven things that will destroy us: wealth without work; pleasure without conscience; knowledge without character; religion without

sacrifice; politics without principle; science without humanity; business without ethics."

— *Mahatma Gandhi*

You don't get to this point overnight. Becoming a person who keeps your word starts with doing the little things, like calling someone back when you say you will or arriving to an appointment on time. Once people know that they can count on you, you will be seen as a person whose word comes to pass. You will come to see yourself that way, too. Eventually, if you make a promise to yourself and to others to make some change in your life or achieve some goal, others will believe that you will do it. Make your word your bond, both to yourself and to others, and you will turn yourself into a person who shapes your own identity by honoring your word.

"Character is much easier kept than recovered."

— *Thomas Paine*

"Be more concerned with your character than your reputation, because your character is what you really are, while your reputation is merely what others think you are."

— *John Wooden*

Action Items

#1: What would your credibility FICO score be today?
____

#2: What are three things you can do immediately to increase your credibility score?

1. _____

2. _____

3. _____

Recommended Videos

What's Worse Than a Bounced Check as an Entrepreneur:

https://www.youtube.com/watch?v=thbYIxaYXBU

What's More Important: Your Face, Name, or Message:
https://www.youtube.com/watch?v=aAD5_MEpZqE

Law 4: Strengthening Your Greatest Weapon

WHY SHOULD WE STOP LEARNING when we finish school at age eighteen or twenty-two, or at age fifty, or ever? It's funny that we accept that going to college will lead to making more money or getting a better career yet we don't assume that self-education will increase our success potential. You don't need a teacher and a university to learn. As a matter of fact, we live in a world where you can have access to just about any book, article, audio file, or video that you want with the click of a mouse. And you can have access to all that information all the time on your tablet, eReader, or smartphone. You can educate yourself on history, matters of money, personal development, or just about anything that you want.

"A room without books is like a body without a soul."

— Marcus Tullius Cicero

When I was young I did not like to read, nor did I think that reading was cool. Up through the age of eighteen, I had read only two books cover to cover: That Was Then, This is Now by S.E. Hinton and Of Mice and Men by John Steinbeck. I was the kid in high school who thought people who read books were nerds.

After I was discharged from the military, I wanted to do something great with my life, but I didn't know where to start. A mentor of mine told me that leaders are readers. On his advice, I started reading, and then I couldn't stop. I have read over 1000 books cover to cover. Before I got married, I read books on marriage. Before starting my business, I read books by great business leaders. Anything I want to know more about or get better at, I read a book on. Now, fifteen years later, I have turned into the book nerd that I used to make fun of.

"One hour per day of study will put you at the top of your field within three years. Within five years you'll be a national authority. In seven years, you can be one of the best

people in the world at what you do."

— Earl Nightingale 1921-1989, Author and Speaker

Reading allows you to shape your identity independently of your current circumstances. You internalize the wisdom and knowledge of the authors who you read. They say that there are two types of experiences that we can learn and grow from: personal experience and the experience that we borrow from others. Reading allows you to learn from mentors who you don't have access to in your daily life. Learning from other people's stories of challenges and triumph is far less painful and time-consuming than going through those challenges yourself. That is why most of the world's greatest leaders have been avid readers.

> *"One should never stop being trained. That is a victory."* — *Sun Tzu*

Action Items

#1: Find a couple of books that have something to teach you or that inspire you. Every morning when you get up and every night before you go to bed, read for just fifteen minutes. You can get a list of books that I recommend at http://www.patrickbetdavid.com/top-100-books/.

I probably couldn't tell you a single song on the Billboard charts right now. The reality is that I don't listen to the radio much. I listen to CDs that teach me principles to build my identity. I listen to inspirational stories, biographies, and experts on finance and business. I listen and I learn.

Odds are, if you live in a big city, you spend a lot of time in traffic. Most of us spend at least one hour per day driving. That's 365 hours per year of potential education time. There is a wealth of knowledge available today through books on CD, podcasts, and educational radio. There's nothing wrong with listening to music—I love music—but ask yourself if you might trade in some of your music time for some learning and growing.

#2: In your car for the next thirty days, do not listen to anything other than inspirational CDs or biographies of great achievers. Put it to the test and see how you change in thirty days. Share your experience with us on Facebook: https://www.facebook.com/PatrickBetDavid.Valuetainment/

Recommended Videos

How to Read a Book a Day:

https://www.youtube.com/watch?v=k7Ev6jor4Ug

10 Commandments of Reading:

http://www.patrickbetdavid.com/the-ten-commandments-of-reading/

Law 5: Challenging Your Way of Thinking

SOMETIMES HITTING THE LOWEST POINT in our lives can be the turning point that causes us to challenge and change our current ways of thinking. I remember clearly that low point in my own life. It was in late 1999 to early 2000. I was nearly $50,000 in debt. I had twenty-six different credit cards and my credit score was around 490. I was at rock bottom financially, emotionally, spiritually, and in my relationships. I felt like nothing in my life was going right. It seemed that all forces were aligned against me. Pretty much everything and everyone was to blame, except my own decisions.

It was there in my darkest hour that something occurred to me that changed my life. I realized that it was my way of thinking that had gotten me to where I was, not some set of outside forces that I couldn't control. It didn't take a long time for me to realize that

I had to change my way of thinking or else life was going to be the same, if not worse, for a very long time.

> *"You cannot solve a problem with the same level of thinking that created it."*
>
> — *Albert Einstein*

The first thing I did was accept responsibility for my results (or lack thereof). I realized that while I couldn't control the universe, I could control my own actions and my responses to things that happened. The second thing I did was to allow myself to imagine a better future, with the understanding that I could change to become the person who I envisioned.

I remember hearing once that the difference between successful people and unsuccessful people are the questions that they ask themselves. Successful people ask, "What if my dream can become a reality? What if I can achieve the impossible? What if I can design my own future?" Unsuccessful people ask themselves, "What if I fail? What if something bad happens? What if I am not capable?" If you want to change your answers, first change your questions. The right questions will lead to a motivation to follow through on the answers. Your mind will find a way to make what you imagine a reality once you accept that you are not only responsible for but are also capable of making that future a reality.

"The world we have created is a product of our thinking; it cannot be changed without changing our thinking."

— Albert Einstein

Action Items

#1: Write down five "what if" questions that would motivate you to change your thinking. Then allow yourself to envision that possibility as reality. Examples: "What if I got in the best shape of my life?" "What if I started my own business?" "What if I ran for public office?" "What if I had $500,000 in the bank?"

1. _____

2. _____

3. _____

4. _____

5. _____

If you view your "what ifs" as challenges to overcome, you must start by upgrading your thinking to the level that can accomplish those challenges. The books you read, the mentors who you listen to, and the associations that you make all change your level of thinking. As a matter of fact, reading this book is designed to change the way you think. In the "empires of the mind," the future is designed mentally before it can be created physically.

Challenging your way of thinking means constantly imagining new possibilities, stretching your belief, and daring to try something new.

#2: Make a list of five areas in your life in which you can challenge and change your thinking. Examples might be the way you look at money, commitment, hard work, being a business owner, success, your faith, exercise, politics, etc.

1. _____

2. _____

3. _____

4. _____

5. _____

Recommended Videos

10 Different Roles Within a Company:

http://www.patrickbetdavid.com/roles-within-a-company/

The One Thing Small Thinkers Master:

http://www.patrickbetdavid.com/small-thinkers-master/

How To Break the Curse of Your Limiting Beliefs:

http://www.patrickbetdavid.com/how-to-break-the-curse-of-your-limiting-beliefs/

Law 6: Know Your "Why"

If your why is strong enough, the how doesn't matter.

THE MOST COMMON ANSWER I get when I ask people why they work is to pay their bills. What an empty reason to work! The great ones do what they do for their whys. They won't and can't give up because their why is that strong.

For the past ten years I have said that mankind is lazy until something catches his heart. You have to know what you are fighting for. Your why is what fuels your life. If you don't have a clear picture of your why to get you through the times when you are tired, over-whelmed, or disappointed, you will run out of gas before you get there. Remember, our natural state is to be lazy and to take the path of least resistance, unless we are motivated by the why in our heart. The bigger your goal, the more powerful your why must be.

Consider the story of two friends, Big Mike and Little Mike:

> Big Mike and Little Mike have been best friends and neighbors their entire lives. Big Mike plays football for his school, but he is very lazy. His coach searches in vain for a way to motivate him and tap into his potential, but Big Mike seems content to do the bare minimum and ride the bench. Then one day after practice, Little Mike is hit by a car right in front of Big Mike and dies in his arms. The coach expects that Big Mike will need to take some time off from football to mourn the loss of his best friend. But just the opposite happens. Monday morning comes and Big Mike is on the field early, putting 110% into practice. Friday night's big game comes and Big Mike asks his coach to start him in the game. He plays like his life depends on it; he gets six sacks, four interceptions, and the winning touchdown. At the end of the game, Big Mike's coach comes up to him and says, "What happened to you? I have never seen you play like that." Big Mike explains that it was the first game that Little Mike ever got to watch him play. You see, Little Mike was blind and Big Mike wanted to play a great game for his friend looking down on him from heaven. Little Mike was the why that lit the fire under Big Mike.

Could someone know exactly what they want and why they want it and still do nothing about it? The answer is yes. It will all come down to how badly they want it! That's what separates those who make it in the history books from those who do not.

So the real question is what is your why? What has caught your heart? Is it your wife, husband, son, daughter, mother, or father? Or just the simple fact that you want to make a difference in this world before your time is up? Why is transformative. You'll start hearing people tell you things like, "I don't recognize you anymore." That's the beginning of the most exciting years of your life because you've made the shift towards truly changing your future.

> "A champion needs motivation above and beyond wining."
>
> — Pat Riley

Action Item

What's your why? What are three reasons or people in your life worth fighting for?

1. _____

2. _____

3. _____

Recommended Videos

The Evolution of Your Why:

http://www.patrickbetdavid.com/evolution-of-your-why/

26 Reasons to become an Entrepreneur:

http://www.patrickbetdavid.com/reasons-to-become-an-entrepreneur/

Law 7: Work Like It's 1880

WE HAVE ALL HEARD THE EXPRESSION "work smarter, not harder." The reality is that you can't substitute working smart for working hard; you have to do both. It is important to work smart, and that comes from experience and wisdom; but who has convinced us that there is such a thing as an easy path to success?

If you go to the book store today you will see all kinds of books promising a shortcut for success: "Lose 30 Pounds in 30 Days," "The 4-Hour Work Day," "Fix Your Marriage in These Five Easy Steps." We are told that if we just click on this website we will find our soulmate waiting for us. In business, relationships, sports, or anything else, there is no instant trick that will substitute for hard work and consistent dedication. Maybe you can lose thirty pounds in thirty days; but without hard work, you won't keep the weight off. There is no magic pill that will allow you to lounge around all day and eat pizza and potato chips and simultaneously stay in shape. There is no five step program to transform your marriage overnight. There is no such thing as a successful plan to "get rich quick." All these things take consistent effort.

"A mind always employed is always happy."

— Thomas Jefferson

One of the biggest challenges facing American prosperity is the loss of work ethic. It seems that there is a taboo against working beyond nine to five in this country. But it wasn't always that way. When I studied the history of the work day in the United States of America, I was shocked to see how it has dwindled over time and been replaced by drastic increases in leisure time.

"Blessed is the person who is too busy to worry in the day- time and too sleepy to worry at night."

— Unknown

According to the US Department of the Interior (2), our hours worked have drastically decreased over the past 200 years:

Year	Average Hours Worked per Week
1830	69.1
1900	58.5
1929	50
Today	39.2

Year	Lifetime Hours of Leisure
1880	43,000
Today	200,000

Division of the Day for the Average Male Household Head over the Course of a Year, 1880 and 1995:

Activity	1880	1995
Sleep	8	8
Meals and hygiene	2	2
Chores	2	2
Travel to and from work	1	1
Work	8.5	4.7
Illness	.7	.5
Leisure activities	1.8	5.8

Estimated Trend in the Lifetime Distribution of Discretionary Time, 1880–2040:

Activity	1880	1995	2040
Lifetime Discretionary	225,900	298,500	321,900
Lifetime Work Hours	182,100	122,400	75,900
Lifetime Leisure Hours	43,800	176,100	246,000

If you look at any great achiever, he didn't allow himself to be constrained by the idea of an eight-hour work day. Consider what Thomas Edison said towards the end of his life after the idea of the eight-hour work day had been introduced into American life:

> "I am wondering what would have happened to me if some fluent talker had converted me to the theory of the eight-hour day and convinced me that it was not fair to my fellow workers to put forth my best efforts in my work. I am glad that the eight-hour day had not been invented when I was a young man. If my life had been made up of eight-hour days, I do not believe I could have accomplished a great deal. This country would not amount to as much as it does if the young men of fifty years ago had been afraid that they might earn more than they were paid for."

Looking at the numbers, it becomes obvious that we have replaced many work hours with leisure hours. Part of the reason for the increase in recreation over work is that we have so many entertainment options competing for our attention today: video games, social media, television, movies, professional sports— the list goes on. According the Government Bureau of Labor Statistics (3), Americans spend an average of 2.8 hours per day watching television.

People that know me know what a sports fan I am. I once went seven years without missing a single Lakers game. One day I realized that by following the dreams of the Lakers with such dedication, I was sacrificing focus on my own dreams. We get so wrapped up in the dreams of the American Idol contestants or the lives of the Kardashians that we let them replace our own story and our own goals.

> *"The dictionary is the only place that success comes before hard work. Hard work is the price we must pay for success. I think you can accomplish anything if you are willing to pay the price."*
>
> — *Vince Lombardi*

We are told that we need to get at least eight hours of sleep per night. But I find that the more I sleep, the more I yawn. We are told to get rest and relax when we are under the weather. But I find that when I am sick and I stay in bed, my sickness lasts longer than when I force myself to go to the gym, work out, and sweat it out in the sauna.

If you are reading this book, you probably want to do something big with your life. This just doesn't happen with an eight-hour work day. You have to be willing to do the hard work and the smart work if you want to reach for a big dream.

A good place to look for examples of the power of hard work is in the world of sports. Two football greats, Jerry Rice and Emmett Smith, are remembered not just for their talent, but for their extreme work ethic. Emmitt Smith said, "For me, winning isn't something that happens suddenly on the field when the whistle blows and the crowds roar. Winning is something that builds physically and mentally every day that you train and every night that you dream." John Madden once said of Jerry Rice, "That work ethic is what makes Jerry Rice so special. He's not only better than any of the other wide receivers; he works harder than any of the others. You don't see that combination too often: where the guy that's the best also works the hardest."

I love the true story of Chris Gardner that was portrayed in the movie The Pursuit of Happyness starring Will Smith. Gardner is the perfect example of the transformative power of hard work. Gardner went from being homeless and broke, raising a young son in shelters and soup kitchens, to being the owner of a very successful brokerage firm in a matter of a few years. He did it by sheer persistence and work ethic— by being the first to the office and the last to leave, by making the amount of client calls in a day that other brokers made in a week. If you haven't seen the movie The Pursuit of Happyness, I highly recommend it.

One of the greatest things about this country is that anyone can make it big with dedication and hard work. We call it "the American Dream." The first immigrants to the United States were often those who wanted to escape the class system in their country for a shot at success in America based on ability, hard work, and innovation. Americans have always been dreamers, but we must also remain hard workers. Dreams without hard work are nothing more than fantasies.

Action Items

#1.　　How many hours a week do you spend on the following?

	Hours
Sleep	
Work	
TV Time	
Exercise	
Eating	
Driving	
Leisure activities	
Reading	
Family time	

#2. How would you rate yourself from one to ten when it comes down to your work ethic?___

#3. What are three things you do to in order to be more efficient with your time?

1. _____

2. _____

3. _____

Recommended Videos

It Takes 7-10 Years to Build:
http://www.patrickbetdavid.com/years-to-build/

Can You Die from Hard Work?:

https://www.youtube.com/watch?v=y75QDTI0OyM
&t

Law 8: Elevate Imagination to a Whole New Level

IMAGINATION IS ONE OF THE THINGS that separates humans from all other living creatures: the ability to see things not as they are but as we imagine they can be. Have you really taken the time to think about the role that imagination plays in your life? Is it a gift or a muscle that can be built with exercise? Where has your imagination taken you?

Think about the imagination that allowed George Lucas to create the universe of Star Wars, or J.K. Rowling to dream up an entire world of wizardry for Harry Potter. Writers and directors by their very nature have powerful imaginations that they cultivate in their art. These books and movies have a powerful effect on our emotions because our own imaginations allow our minds to treat the fantasy as reality. Have you ever noticed what happens to you when you watch certain movies? Think about how you feel after watching Rocky. Does a part of you feel like you are in the ring with "The Italian Stallion," fighting to be a champion? How about when you watch The Notebook? I'm sure no man reading this has ever watched that movie (isn't that right, guys?), so let me fill you in: A powerful love story makes you think about your high school sweetheart, about the first time you met your wife, or about that individual in your imagination who you can't wait to meet.

> *"Imagination is more important than knowledge. For knowledge is limited to all we now know and understand, while imagination embraces the entire world, and all there ever will be to know and understand."*
>
> — *Albert Einstein*

Sometimes the best movies we ever watch are the ones we direct in our own minds. That is the magic of books and movies: The imagination of the creator awakens our own imaginations as we share in his or her fantasy.

> *"I paint objects as I think them, not as I see them."*
>
> — *Pablo Picasso*

But what role does imagination play in our real life?

We can sometimes let our imaginations run away with us, often in the wrong direction:

1. Where does your imagination take you when the phone rings after midnight?

2. What do you imagine when you lend your car to your sixteen-year-old for the first time?

3. Where does your imagination take you when you're walking by yourself late at night and you hear foot- steps behind you?

Still, imagination can do amazing things when we let it run wild in the right direction. Imagination is a critical part of our lives; everything starts with imagination. When we are dating, we picture what it would be like to marry that person before we make the commitment. Before you buy your dream house, you must first envision it. Before you build a business, you must first conceive it in your mind.

"Imagination rules the world."

— Napoleon Bonaparte

Before you do the impossible, you must first imagine it. And just as movie producers and fiction writers bring us into their imagination, our imagination has the power to inspire vision in others.

Let me give you an example:

In 1974, UCLA's basketball team was on an eighty-eight game winning streak. The Bruins seemed unbeatable. Despite overwhelming odds, Notre Dame Coach Digger Phelps had faith that his team could beat the undefeated Bruins. He just needed to make his players believe it.

At the end of the first day of practice the week before the game, Phelps asked his team to imagine how beating UCLA would feel. He told them to celebrate as if they had just won the big game. At first his team gave it a half-hearted effort, perhaps thinking that the exercise was corny or a waste of time. But Coach Phelps persisted and each day after practice the team would celebrate as if they had just beaten the Bruins. By the final practice, the team needed no prompting from their coach. After practice they instantaneously burst into celebration, jumping up and down, yelling and hugging each other with the imagined feeling of victory over their legendary rivals.

> *"The man who has no imagination has no wings."*
>
> — *Muhammad Ali*

By the time of the big game, the Fighting Irish basketball team had envisioned their moment of victory with such passion and clarity that defeat was not an option. Notre Dame scored the last twelve points of the game to defeat top-ranked UCLA 71-70, ending the Bruins' record eighty-eight game domination. They won after they believed they were going to win. They believed it because they imagined it so many times.

Many leaders have used this inspiring story to show the importance of believing in your people, but I see Phelps as a leader who used the gift of imagination to steer the soul of his team towards doing the impossible.

Action Items

Answer the following questions and let your imagination run wild.

1. What would you do with a million dollars?

2. If you could be anyone in the world, who would you want to be? (President? Professional athlete? Movie star? Fortune 100 CEO?)

3. If money were not an issue, what car would you buy?

4. If you could live anywhere, where would it be? What would your house look like?

5. In the future, there is an event being held in your honor. How does the host introduce you?

Recommended Videos

8 Things that Cause Entrepreneurs to be more Creative:

http://www.patrickbetdavid.com/entrepreneurs-to-be-more-creative/

3 Vision Boards for Entrepreneurs:

http://www.patrickbetdavid.com/3-types-vision-boards-entrepreneurs/

Worst Questions to Ask Yourself:

http://www.patrickbetdavid.com/worst-question-ask/

Law 9: Be As Curious As Alice

WE ALL REMEMBER THE STORY of Alice, the curious child whose inquisitive streak led her down a rabbit-hole and into Wonderland. The book explains that Alice had to follow the White Rabbit because she was "burning with curiosity." That same curiosity led Alice to down bottles that said "drink me" and cakes that said "eat me" and enter a strange world that became "curiouser and curiouser." Her desire to uncover every mystery is one of the things that most children reading the story can relate to.

There are some things that we do as children that we unfortunately stop doing as much as adults. Children are constantly learning and growing. They are curious about the world around them and anxious to learn and try new things. Curiosity is a gift from God

that shouldn't disappear when we become adults. Learning is something that is just as important at age seventy as it is at age seven. Too many of us stop asking questions in life as we get older; we simply lose that childlike thirst for knowledge. Part of the reason for that is the fact that we are afraid of being embarrassed, looking foolish or ruffling feathers. But at the end of the day, the worst question is one that is never asked.

> *"Intellectual growth should commence at birth and cease only at death."*
>
> — *Albert Einstein*

Curiosity is not just about learning new facts or information. The great ones don't just want to learn; they want to learn to do. They become students of those who do things better or differently and learn what those people know. Once they have one thing down, they move onto something new, always learning, ever evolving their abilities.

Let me give you a great real world example: Kobe Bryant.

When Kobe Bryant first came into the league, he wanted to learn every part of the game: foot work, outside shot, defense, closing, turn-around shot, posting up, and every other tool of the game. Kobe was a great player even then and a sought-after draft pick.

However, critics thought that he made a mistake by not playing college ball to refine his game before going to the NBA. But Kobe understood that he didn't know everything, and he became one of the best students ever to play in the NBA. While his peers and competitors were excited just to be in the pros, Kobe wanted to be the greatest of all time. One of the biggest differences between Kobe and other players who enter the NBA is the fact that Kobe has never stopped learning.

> *"Judge a man by his questions rather than by his answers."*
>
> *— Voltaire*

Even after establishing himself as one of the great ones in the NBA, Kobe kept evolving his skill set. In 2009, with four championship rings already on his finger, Kobe went to Hakeem Olajuwon to master his footwork. Here's what Kobe said about working with Hakeem Olajuwon: "I got a chance to work with the greatest post player ever. I've always been a student of the game, and he was very patient with me." Phil Jackson said of Kobe's drive to learn, "Kobe always comes back with a goal, he doesn't go through summer playing golf or going fishing. He's got some- thing in his mind he's going to work on with his game during the offseason."

> *"Curiosity is the wick in the candle of learning."*
>
> *— William Arthur Ward*

Kobe Bryant is just one example. Steve Wozniak and Steve Jobs kept asking "what if" questions that first enabled and then revolutionized personal computing. The secrets of the universe or the secrets of better foot- work and everything in between are all available to those who want to learn. You just have to start with the desire to learn and grow. Then get in touch with your inner Alice. Ask why and how and who can I learn from? The great thing about curiosity is that it doesn't ever need to be satisfied; you can keep learning and trying new things as long as you live.

Action Items

What are some areas of your life where you can use your gift of curiosity to increase your learning?

1. _____

2. _____

3. _____

Recommended Videos

Visionary or Phony? How to Tell Them Apart:

https://www.youtube.com/watch?v=DS8HTo-b2g0&

Why Most Entrepreneurs Fail:

http://www.patrickbetdavid.com/why-most-entrepreneurs-fail/

Law 10: Break Away From The Old You

THERE ARE TWO TYPES OF PEOPLE in the world: those who wait and those who do. Those who wait spend most of their lives in the planning stage, getting ready to do something. They talk about their dreams in terms of "someday." Those who wait are waiting for that perfect moment when all the stars align for them to go after their dreams. They say things like "I will do it … after my kids are older … when I have enough money … when I have more time." The reality is that "someday" never comes and the person who waits misses every opportunity while holding out for that perfect moment.

Doers understand that time flies. We get one shot at life. Whatever it is that you want to do with it, don't wait until the opportunities pass you by. We never feel completely ready for life's big decisions; but in taking the leap, we push ourselves to the next level.

It's funny how sometimes having nothing to lose gives you the motivation to make a big change. In March of

1997 my mother moved back to Iran. My father had had a heart attack a few years earlier and was in poor health. I was on my third job and attending Glendale Community College. I had to sell my Chevy S10 for

$1700.00 just to afford a place to live for a month with my sister. So my mom left me her Toyota Corolla to use while she was in Iran. One day I went out to the curb to get in the car and it wasn't there.

> *"Do not wait; the time will never be just right. Start where you stand, and work with whatever tools you may have at your command, and better tools will be found as you go along."*
>
> *— Napoleon Hill*

Something about getting my car stolen when I was already struggling pushed me into an immediate decision. I had dreamed of joining the Army since I was fourteen, but I had put off enlisting when I graduated high school. That very moment, I called my dad and asked him to drive me to the Army recruiting station in Glendale, California. The Army wanted me to wait months to enter basic training; but I pushed, and within two weeks I was in boot camp in South Carolina.

That split second decision that I made to join the Army turned out to be the best path that I could have chosen at that point in my life. The Army challenged me, built my character, and helped shape my identity into what it is today. The lesson is that sometimes the best decisions that we make are ones that we make before we feel ready. Procrastination is just a word for taking the time to talk yourself out of something.

I remember one day I was talking to a very successful mentor of mine and he asked me when I planned to get married. I told him that I wanted to wait until I was financially stable. My mentor looked at me and said, "Patrick, we are never fully ready for the big decisions in life, whether that's getting married, having kids, or starting a business."

Consider the words General George Patton wrote in his diary on November 6, 1942, right before a pivotal battle in World War II:

> *"In forty hours I shall be in battle, with little information, and on the spur of the moment will have to make most momentous decisions, but I believe that one's spirit enlarges with responsibility and that, with God's help, I shall make them and make them right. It seems my whole life has been leading up to this moment."*

Patton said that "one's spirit enlarges with opportunity." He didn't know what was going to happen once the battle started. All of his training and preparation could not guarantee the outcome or circumstances. But he took a leap of faith, believing in his purpose and that with Divine support he would be able to make the right tactical decisions as they came. Doers enlarge their spirit by taking on more responsibility, going after new challenges, and crossing into unchartered territory.

> *"Things do come to those who wait, but only those things left over from those who hustle."*
>
> — *Abraham Lincoln*

Action Items

#1. What are three good habits you have that have served you in your life?

1. _____

2. _____

3. _____

#2. What are three bad habits you can break away from to help recreate yourself?

1. _____

2. _____

3. _____

Recommended Videos

8 Personality Traits that Repel Good People:

http://www.patrickbetdavid.com/8personalitytraits/

Never let a Resume Fool You:

http://www.patrickbetdavid.com/never-let-resume-fool/

10 Laws on How to Recreate Yourself:

http://www.patrickbetdavid.com/10-laws-on-how-to-recreate-yourself/

How to Start a New Life:

http://www.patrickbetdavid.com/best-motivational-video-how-to-start-a-new-life/

Morning Rituals of an Entrepreneur:

http://www.patrickbetdavid.com/morning-rituals-of-an-entrepreneur/

Law 11: Decide to Be the Chosen One

BEING A "CHOSEN ONE" doesn't mean that your name is Jesus and you can walk on water; that's not what this chapter is about. It's about being someone with a calling to be the hero, someone with a higher purpose. Those who do the impossible want to be the chosen ones. They desire to be the solution to the problem. They thrive on people relying on them. They enjoy delivering on their promises. They seek out responsibility. This mentality might not make sense to every- one, but this is one of the things that makes the chosen ones different.

There are twelve guys on a basketball roster, but the chosen one is the player who wants the ball when the team is down two points with only four seconds left to play in the championship game. If he makes the shot he gets the all the glory, the praise, and the press. But if he misses the shot, he gets the crowds disappointment and the feeling of letting his team down. You see, being the chosen one in any arena comes with a price.

Imagine the pressure in an NBA championship game to make that winning shot. Most people will never feel the burden or the glory of shooting the winning basket in the NBA. But we have the opportunity to be the hero in other ways. This country, our economy, and a lot of families are facing challenging times. When times are hard, heroes rise up. Tough times don't create heroes, but challenges reveal the hero inside of us. Even though a chosen one will get the glory, that isn't their number one motivation. A hero or chosen one wants to make an impact and leave a legacy. He has a sense of responsibility to a cause.

> *"A hero is an ordinary individual who finds the strength to*
>
> *persevere and endure in spite of overwhelming obstacles."*
>
> *— Christopher Reeve*

When I go speaking all across the country, I hear a lot of people ask things like, "Can one person really make a difference?" My response is very simple. Did Martin Luther King, Billy Graham, Albert Einstein, Alexander Graham Bell, or Thomas Edison make a difference? Did the people who knew these men before they achieved greatness know that that they were one day going to become such heroes? Did they see them as the person who is talked about on television, written about in books, and quoted by thousands worldwide?

Christopher Reeve is a great example of someone who decided to be the chosen one in his battle against spinal cord injury. He recognized his opportunity to use his fame and his injury to help the thousands that suffer from paralysis. He made his crusade about much more than his own personal struggle. Even beyond the death of Reeve himself, the Christopher Reeve Foundation continues to have a profound impact on awareness, funding, research, and education for victims of spinal cord injury.

> *"A hero is someone who has given his or her life to some- thing bigger than oneself."*
>
> *— Joseph Campbell*

I believe we're at a time in this country where we're counting on many people all across the nation to decide to be the chosen ones of their generation. This country is looking for the next generation of heroes. They're not all going to be in the same industry; they'll be in technology, science, sports, politics, education, finance, the church, the military, local communities, and many other places.

What is your cause? If you decide to become the chosen one, what are you "chosen" to do? This book is not about telling you what your crusade should be. That has to be a personal decision based on the fire inside of you. Have a clear picture of what you feel chosen to do and make that your purpose. Your life will never be the same, and it will be more exhilarating than you can imagine.

Action Item

Imagine that one hundred years from now your picture is on the wall of your great-grandkid's home. What would you want them to say about you?

_____

_____

_____

_____

_____

Recommended Videos

5 Identities of an Entrepreneur:

http://www.patrickbetdavid.com/identities-of-an-entrepreneur/

10 Unmeasurable Qualities of a Human Being:

http://www.patrickbetdavid.com/unmeasurable-qualities-human-beings/

Law 12: Go "All In" with One Industry

WE ARE LIVING IN TIMES where everyone is looking for the latest and greatest thing. But if you look at history, whether one hundred years ago or ten years ago, the great ones all devoted their passion to one thing and stuck with it. The reality is that if you try to do too many things, you will do none of them very well. The great ones are not those who pursue every opportunity or try everything that interests them. They are dedicated to a path and they are not distracted by every new, shiny object that catches their eye.

In poker, going "all in" is when you bet all your chips on one hand. It can be a sign of how strong your hand is, or it can be a bluff; but either way, the player is 100% committed to that hand. Becoming one of the greats at anything means being willing to put all your chips in the pot and make that industry your "all in" moment.

> *"Think enthusiastically about everything, but especially about your job. If you do so, you'll put a touch of glory in your life."*
>
> — *Norman Vincent Peale*

When you think about Michael Jordan, one sport comes to mind. Jordan dedicated himself to basketball and become one of the best players in NBA history. At one point, Jordan took a break from basketball to go back to his favorite childhood sport of baseball. It didn't work out very well.

Just like a successful marriage means going all in with one person for the rest of your life, being great at something means marrying that industry or activity. Donald Trump married real estate. Steve Jobs put all his chips into Apple and innovative consumer technology products. Mohammed Ali went all in with boxing. He didn't quit in the middle of his career to try his hand at football. Those who choose to do the impossible don't commit to their path for five years; they commit for twenty years, or for life.

> *"I'm committed to one company. This is the industry I've decided to work in."*
>
> — *Bill Gates*

When I got out of the Army in 1999, I had no clue what I was going to do. I started working at a Bally's Total Fitness health club. I learned very quickly that the industry of sales has no limit to how well you can do.

Still, I wanted to find an industry that I could go all in with. I met a mentor of mine in Newport Beach, California, who showed me the value of the financial services industry and I have never looked back. I may do other things (like write a book on how to do the impossible), but financial services is my industry; we got married eleven years ago and our organization is committed to becoming the Yankees, Apple, Google, or Wal-Mart of the financial industry.

"The wise man puts all his eggs in one basket and watches the basket."

— Andrew Carnegie

Being great at anything takes time, commitment, and consistency. We all know those people that join every-thing—the person who tells you how excited he is about an opportunity in the travel industry, and six months later he is selling you on the newest, greatest weight-loss product.

The great ones first choose an industry, then they commit to it 100%. They want to develop something that is around long after they are gone. Alexander the Great only lived thirty-three years, but here we are still talking about him 2,300 years later. If you want to build a legacy that will outlive you by centuries, commit to your path, for better or worse, in sickness and in health, 'til death do you part.

Action Items

#1: Do you catch yourself being bored with what you do?

_____

#2: What industry do you want to go all in with, and why?

Industry:_____
Why:_____
_____
_____

Recommended Videos

Goals vs Vision: What's more Important?:

https://www.youtube.com/watch?v=FLnc3pjVnI4

7 Tips on when to go Full Time:
http://www.patrickbetdavid.com/when-to-go-full-time-as-an-entrepreneur/

3 Steps on How to be Wealthy:
http://www.patrickbetdavid.com/3-steps-on-how-to-be-wealthy/

Law 13: Push the Envelope

THE EXPRESSION "PUSHING THE ENVELOPE" comes from the transition from propeller-driven airplanes to jets. Aircraft designers were reaching into the unknown in terms of new engines, creating very different performance limits compared with the designs of the pre-1948 era. Test pilots who flew beyond what designers and engineers calculated was possible and/ or safe were said to be "pushing the outside of the flight envelope."

Those who want to achieve the impossible understand that to become great, you have to push the envelope. Just like those test pilots, you have to go beyond the limits of what you know you can do and find out what you are capable of.

Accomplishing the impossible in life is a journey with many smaller destinations on the way. The great ones don't get to one goal and then stop. They see each goal met as a stepping stone on the journey to something truly extraordinary.

If you look at anything in life, growth comes from resistance. When you lift weights, your muscles are torn down and rebuilt bigger and stronger. In the same way, our mind, our emotions, and our thinking all grow and are rebuilt through resistance. If you are not experiencing any resistance in your life, you are probably not growing personally or professionally. If you find yourself at a place where everything is routine at work and you are just going through the motions at home, you need to set yourself up to be challenged. Wherever you are professionally, in your marriage, as a parent, spiritually, or as a member of your community, we can all get better at every area of our lives. Are you challenging yourself to get to the next level? Are you working out those muscles with resistance and growing your capabilities?

On October 5, 2011, the world lost one of the great business visionaries of our time: Steve Jobs. What would our world be like if Jobs was satisfied after Apple created the first personal computer? Imagine if Steve Jobs didn't push the envelope. What if he was hesitant when it came down to the big decisions?

What made Jobs extraordinary is that he never rested on his accomplishments. He helped create the first PC, quite an accomplishment in and of itself. But Jobs wasn't done yet. He then revolutionized the music industry with iTunes and the iPod. Still not satisfied, he transformed the smart phone market with the iPhone. And even after he knew he was fighting a losing battle with cancer, Jobs continued to push the envelope, reinventing portable computing with the iPad.

Many companies have faded into irrelevance after one or two breakthroughs; not Apple, though. Steve Jobs boldly led Apple to push the envelope and think outside the realm of current reality. Because of his vision and tenacity, Steve Jobs and Apple created tens of thousands of jobs and billions of dollars in revenue. He did this by coming up with an innovative product that enhances the lives of millions. Then he did it again. And again. And again.

We admire Steve Jobs for his relentless pursuit of the next evolution in technology.

So why should we be any different in our own lives?

Pushing the envelope means not being content with the status quo. It means finding out just how fast your plane can fly and how high it can go.

Action Items

#1. What areas of your life are you content with?

1. _____

2. _____

3. _____

#2: What are some things you can do to push the envelope in order to take it to the next level?

1. _____

2. _____

3._____

Recommended Videos

Self-Confidence- You vs You:

http://www.patrickbetdavid.com/self-confidence/

10 Ways Competition Helps You Win in Business:

http://www.patrickbetdavid.com/compete-in-business/

Law 14: Turn Your Cause into a Crusade

SOMETIMES ON THE WAY TO A DREAM you get lost and find a bigger one.

The dictionary defines a crusade as "a vigorous, aggressive movement for the defense or advancement of an idea, cause, etc."

If you look at the great ones throughout history, they all had something that they were fighting for that went beyond their own personal reward. Those who do the impossible rarely, if ever, do it for the money. Those who are motivated by money are the ones who slow down when they get to their target income level, while those who keep going are motivated by something more than wealth. To them, their business is a cause, a movement, a crusade.

Every time I visit a cemetery I am reminded that we are all mortal. What we do in the eighty or so years that we get on this planet will determine what we leave behind and how we are remembered. Those who are driven by money alone will be forgotten, but those who use the gifts that God gave them to change the world are remembered indefinitely.

I remember clearly the day we finally escaped Iran to come to America. It was November 28, 1990. It was one of the greatest days of my life. But America wasn't something that I thought of as being handed to me outright. I wanted to earn the right to be able to live in a nation as special as America.

"You lose nothing when fighting for a cause. In my mind the quitters are those who don't have a cause they care about."

— Muhammad Ali

In March of 2009, I was at a dinner party at the Miramar Hotel and I heard George Will give a speech about America. Mr. Will explained that this generation needs to get its act together in order for us as a nation to keep our freedom. He shared a quote from Ronald Reagan that moved me in a way that very few quotes have:

"Freedom is never more than one generation away from extinction. We didn't pass it to our children in the bloodstream. It must be fought for, protected, and handed on for them to do the same, or one day we will spend our sunset years telling our children and our children's children what it was once like in the United States where men were free."

I took what George Will and Ronald Reagan said personally. The way I see it, it's very simple: I believe that I have a responsibility to stand up for a cause. I didn't come to America just to live "the American Dream." The leadership of PHP didn't just want to build a successful financial services company. We want to lead a crusade to empower individuals to take control of their money and their financial future. We want to inspire a new generation of leaders to reignite America's entrepreneurial spirit. That is our mission. This is why when you sit down with the key leaders of PHP, they inspire you to do things you never thought were possible.

Greatness comes from finding work that isn't merely a job to you; rather, greatness comes from finding work that is a cause within you. When your work becomes a crusade, you will go to sleep Sunday night excited to work on Monday. There's no feeling like it. Whether it's fighting for a different future for this country or a different future for your family, when a cause catches your heart, there is no limit to what you can accomplish. Fighting for a cause bigger than yourself alone not only motivates you: It also inspires those around you. Every great achiever in history has inspired others. That is why we are still talking about Winston Churchill, Martin Luther King, and Abraham Lincoln today. Their achievements were incredible in and of themselves, but how many leaders since then have been inspired and motivated by what those men did?

People are drawn to leaders who believe in changing the world around them. If you fight for a crusade, others will join you. Legacies are never built by just one person. All great leaders have great teams supporting them. Inspire your team, your family, your associates, and your friends with your crusade. Your inspiration will have a positive impact on others' belief in themselves as well.

Action Items

#1: Is there a crusade or a cause behind what you do?

#2: If yes, why do you think that is?

Recommended Videos

How to Grow Your Business Exponentially:

http://www.patrickbetdavid.com/how-to-grow-your-business-exponentially/

3 Ways Leaders Create a Following:

http://www.patrickbetdavid.com/3-ways-leaders-create-a-following/

How to Start a Movement:
http://www.patrickbetdavid.com/how-to-create-a-movement/

Law 15: Channel Your Obsession

EVERY ONE OF US HAS a bit of an obsessive personality. Don't believe me? Ask yourself if you've ever done any of the following or something similar:

1. If you have kids, do you notice that you are constantly thinking about them throughout the day, no matter what you are doing?

2. Do you ever catch yourself watching ESPN Sports Center over and over again knowing it's the same highlights coming up?

3. Do you check for new email on your phone every five minutes, even when you are on vacation?

4. Do you have thirty pairs of shoes but you're still excited about shopping for the next pair?

5. Do you constantly think about what you can do to make your car faster?

6. Are you a person who checks your Facebook or Twitter ten times a day for updates?

7. Do you stay up until 1:00 am to beat the last level of your favorite video game?

We all have obsessions in life. The difference is that those who do the impossible get obsessed with something productive that can make an impact. It's not necessarily that they are more obsessive than everyone else; they just channel that focus into a project or goal to change their lives and the world around them.

> "If experts say you have ADHD use that God-given gift to ignore naysayers. Learn to use your crutches in life as secret weapons."
>
> — Patrick Bet-David

As a young adult, I made a decision to channel my obsession into reading. If my high school buddies could see me now, they'd be shocked that the guy who wouldn't even read the CliffsNotes to a book in high school now reads dozens of books a year.

I've never been a big fan of teachers telling parents that their kids have Attention Deficit Hyperactivity Disorder (ADHD) or Obsessive Compulsive Disorder (OCD) and automatically getting doctors to put them on medication. If you study the people who have invented breakthroughs and changed the world, many of them would be diagnosed with ADHD or OCD. Kids get obsessed with building model airplanes or accessorizing their Barbie doll. That focus and tenacity can be a positive thing later in life. The Wright Brothers were obsessed with flight; Mozart was obsessed with creating music. What we call a disorder today was likely the same trait that made possible many great achievements.

Psychology Today (4) reported that people with ADHD are 300% more likely to become entrepreneurs. Here is a list of famous people you may recognize who have been diagnosed with ADD/ADHD or OCD. Did their obsessive or hyperactive personalities actually contribute to their success? Many say it did. Many of the people on the list did not have their disorders diagnosed until much later in life. Several of them decided to forgo medication and to view their disorder as a positive factor rather than a negative one.

ADD/ADHD

- Justin Timberlake

- Will Smith

- Glenn Beck

- Michael Phelps

- Jim Carrey

- Sir Richard Branson (Founder of Virgin Airlines)

- Terry Bradshaw

- Paul Orfalea (Founder of Kinko's)

- Pete Rose

- David Neeleman (Founder of JetBlue)

- Bruce Jenner

OCD

- Howard Hughes

- Donald Trump

- Cameron Diaz

- Leonardo DiCaprio

- Michael Jackson

- Harrison Ford

- Howard Stern

- Ludwig Van Beethoven

- Albert Einstein

- Michelangelo

- David Beckham

- Sir Winston Churchill

- Martin Scorsese

"I know quite certainly that I myself have no special talent; curiosity, obsession and dogged endurance, combined with self-criticism, have brought me to my ideas."

— *Albert Einstein*

Sometimes a little obsession or hyperactivity, pointed in the right direction, is a vital part of achieving the impossible.

Action Items

#1: What three things are you obsessed with in life? Are they positive or negative obsessions?

Obsession	Positive/Negative

#2: What's one positive thing you can get obsessed with?

Recommended Videos

How to Go from a Street Hustler to an Entrepreneur: https://www.youtube.com/watch?v=lAmscY8caQU

How to Stay Focused as an Entrepreneur:

http://www.patrickbetdavid.com/how-to-stay-focused-as-an-entrepreneur/

Law 16: Evangelize Your Message

A LOT OF PEOPLE probably assume that being a great communicator is important, but the importance of sales skills might not be as obvious. I'm not talking about the person who goes door to door selling products, although there are many success stories there as well. The skill of salesmanship is used by a politician seeking votes and by a parent convincing a seven-year-old to eat his broccoli.

Success requires the ability to sell yourself, your product or service, or your ideas. Many of the great ones who do the impossible master the art of being evangelical in communicating their message to the world. Their zeal comes out of the belief that their message will have a strong, positive impact on others.

If you look at a great coach, pastor, public figure, or business leader, you will see a great salesperson. One of the things that make them special is the fact that they're able to communicate a message to you, to challenge you, or to persuade you to do something that you wouldn't have done without their influence. This is a skill that's a must to learn if you have plans of doing something big.

I've heard people say things like "I'm not really a salesman" or "I just don't like salespeople." Well, I hate to break it to you, but we are all salespeople. When you were sixteen, did you try to sell your parents on the idea of loaning you their car?

Anyone who has dated knows that courtship is all about sales. A job interview is a process of selling yourself to a potential employer. If you're a parent, you learn how to persuade your kids to do their chores or brush their teeth. We sell all the time in life, on little things and on big things.

The great ones take salesmanship to the next level. They become great communicators of their vision and persuade those around them to see that same vision. This isn't a book on salesmanship, but there are some very good books out there on the art of sales. If you want to accomplish something tremendous, you will need to become a prolific communicator.

Recommended Videos

How to Attract the Best Talent to Your Company as an Entrepreneur:
https://www.youtube.com/watch?v=HTMu9_RZu00

17 Ways to Keep the Talented Leaders in Your Company:
http://www.patrickbetdavid.com/lose-talented-leaders/

The 9 Love Languages of Entrepreneurs:
http://www.patrickbetdavid.com/love-languages-entrepreneurs/

Law 17: Aim for the Moon

IN 1961, PRESIDENT JOHN F. KENNEDY stood before the nation and said, "I believe this nation should commit itself to achieving the goal, before the decade is out, of landing a man on the moon and returning him safely to earth." To put that in perspective, in 1961 America had just successfully launched the first American into space. Up until that point we had failed over and over again. Rocket after rocket had blown up in our faces. The Soviet Union was cleaning our clocks in the space race.

Then after a single success the President says we are going to the moon. What an outrageous statement! Did NASA know how to accomplish this goal? Probably not. Was it possible? Many scientists probably weren't sure. But on Sunday July 20, 1969, Neil

Armstrong put his foot on the moon and declared, "That's one small step for man, one giant leap for mankind." Armstrong's moon walk was the conclusion of a 238,855-mile journey to the moon that started in

1961 with JFK's vision and the commitment to make it a reality.

> *"If I had some idea of a finish line, don't you think I would have crossed it years ago?"*
>
> — *Rich DeVos*

While wearing glasses may help us see the visible, having vision enables us to see the invisible, that which does not yet exist. Vision creates a path in our mind to a future of our own design. Having vision not only keeps us on track, but also shows us where the track is.

Those who accomplish the impossible have a vision past what the eye can see, past even their own lifetimes. Think about some of the business pioneers that we would call visionaries. Henry Ford saw a better way to manufacture, when he envisioned the assembly line. Howard Hughes saw cross-continental travel. Ray Kroc conceived the concept of fast food. Sam Walton first imagined discount retail. Steve jobs and the founders of Apple dreamt up the personal computer and Bill Gates saw an operating system to make using a PC simple for everyone. What all these men had in common was a massive vision that they then dedicated their lives to making a reality.

> *"Where there's no vision, the people perish."*
>
> — *Proverbs 29:18*

It is one thing to start a business with the goal of making money or beating the competition. It is another thing to have a vision that challenges traditional thinking by seeing what doesn't exist. The founders of Apple and Microsoft saw a world where everyone would use a personal computer at a time when computers cost tens of thousands of dollars and were the size of a refrigerator.

> *"You can't predict the future, but you can follow your dreams."*
>
> — *Jay Van Andel*

Of course, those who do the impossible don't just have a massive vision; they implement that vision to make it a reality. I've worked with people who have a vision but are not willing to take action. I used to work with a gentleman who was the greatest public speaker I have ever met in my life, but he never took action; he only talked about taking action. I've also met people who are willing to work hard but who have no clue what they are working hard for.

I can remember my struggle to find the right church to join when I first moved to Los Angeles. I will never forget the first service I attended at the Shepherd of the Hills church; I knew I had found my church home. The person who spoke on that day was Pastor Dudley Rutherford. It didn't take me a long time to make a decision that I wanted him to be a close friend and mentor in my life. In less than twenty years he was able to take the attendance of that church from only a few hundred to thirteen thousand members with the help of his leadership team and his awesome wife, Rene. Pastor Rutherford is now getting ready to build a facility that holds 3,500 people. This comes as no surprise to me because I have come to know him as a visionary who does the work required in order to fulfill the vision.

Part of having a massive vision means achieving your goal and then aiming for the next one. A massive vision doesn't end; it evolves. It grows as you grow and you grow as your vision grows. Think about Apple. They didn't stop at the Apple II and say, "Well, we created the personal computer. I guess we are done here." Apple's vision for personal computing has kept growing for the last thirty years, which is why we now have the iPad 2 and not simply the Apple II.

> *"Vision without action is a daydream. Action without vision is a nightmare."*
>
> *— Japanese Proverb*

Over the past fifty years, hundreds of direct marketing businesses have come and gone, but Amway has remained one of the most successful businesses of all time. The reason that Amway has become the largest and longest lasting direct marketing organization goes back to the fact that its founders, Rich DeVos and Jay Van Andel, started with a massive vision. They were big advocates of free enterprise with a dream of empowering individuals with business-ownership and a shot at "the American Dream." I've never been part of Amway nor have I had a relationship with the founders, but I'm extremely impressed with how they created a new kind of entrepreneurship opportunity that became a model for many other successful direct marketing companies.

"History will be kind to me for I intend to write it."

— *Winston Churchill*

Have a massive vision and you can accomplish that vision. a small vision and you will achieve small things.

___

Action Items

#1: Do you know clearly what you want out of life?

#2. If yes, list five things that you want out of life.

___

1. _____

2. _____

3. _____

4. _____

5. _____

#3: How important is it to you for these things to become a reality? The answer to this question could dictate whether or not history will be kind to you.

Recommended Videos

Hardest Things to Find in Life:

http://www.patrickbetdavid.com/4-hardest-things-find-life/

Challenges Every Entrepreneur Will Face:

http://www.patrickbetdavid.com/challenges-every-entrepreneur-will-face/

How to Negotiate with Billion Dollar Companies:

http://www.patrickbetdavid.com/negotiate-billion-dollar-companies/

Why Most People Give Up on Their Dreams:

https://www.youtube.com/watch?v=SAOtSejGIdE

Law 18: Keep the Faith

FAITH IS THE ABILITY to look beyond the reality of cur- rent circumstances and believe in a future that cannot yet be seen. All of the great ones throughout history have shared a high level of faith. For some, that faith is based on spiritual beliefs; for others, it is simply the ability to feel confident in the outcome before the results are in. Faith lets us believe in what will happen in order to make it happen.

People of faith inspire faith in others. We like being around people with a strong belief in the future. People with a high level of faith tend to create a big following. We look for leaders who share their belief with us that great things will happen.

> *"Faith: A strong or unshakeable belief in something, especially without proof or evidence."*

— World English Dictionary

People with a lot of faith are most needed when we go through challenging times. I remember being in Army boot camp. I was the only Middle Eastern private in the unit. Boot camp was some of the toughest weeks of my life. A typical day started at four in the morning with a ten mile run and 500 push-ups. Afterwards we would sit a classroom that was heated to 115 degrees; if you fell asleep you would be shouted at by your drill sergeant and have to run four miles and then return to class. Some days we would have to march fifteen miles in uniform with fifty pounds on our backs while carrying a semi-automatic machine gun. An adventurous day might include a trip to the gas chamber for us to experience how it feels when your skin is burning and you can't see or breathe. (I'm sure by now you're inspired to join the Army or encourage your kids to enlist.)

It wasn't easy, and I struggled a lot during those weeks. One day, our drill sergeant announced that the five privates with the highest physical training score would go to a weekend men's camp. To us, anything off the base was a vacation.

The men's camp turned out to be a Christian camp, and there was a man there who shared with us from the Bible. I couldn't wait for him to finish so I could go play billiards or visit the lake. I had never been a big man of faith. Growing up in a war-torn country, having to leave our family behind, and struggling through poverty all made me doubt that there could be a loving God who would allow those things to happen.

On the last day of camp, when we were getting ready to leave, the man pulled me aside and gave me the Bible that was given to him when he was not yet a believer. He encouraged me to read the Bible and pray. He said, "Life hasn't been the best to you, but maybe it's because God is planning something really special for you and he's trying to toughen you up." That man planted a seed of faith in my life, first by making me believe that everything was going to be alright and then by making me consider that some- thing great could happen.

I believe the highest level of confidence comes from knowing that a higher power is with you through- out your entire journey. That faith has allowed me to accomplish things that I never thought possible ten years ago.

Those who do the impossible eventually develop such a high level of faith that they simply know that every- thing is going to be as they imagine. It's like the stars are aligned in their favor or God is on their side. It's not something that can be explained unless you've experienced it. It's the high level of certainty that they have. They simply believe they're destined to do something incredible in their lives and they're confident that everything will work out. Even when things don't go their way, they look at it as a challenge given to them to make them grow.

Action Items

#1: Do you often doubt yourself? Yes or no.
_____

If yes, why?

_____

#2: What are three things you're willing to commit to in order to increase your level of faith in yourself and your life?

    1. _____

    2. _____

    3. _____

Recommended Videos

How to Become a Born Again Entrepreneur:

http://www.patrickbetdavid.com/become-born-entrepreneur/

Worst Questions to Ask Yourself:

http://www.patrickbetdavid.com/worst-question-ask/

10 Reasons to Never Give Up:

http://www.patrickbetdavid.com/10-reasons-why-you-should-never-give-up/

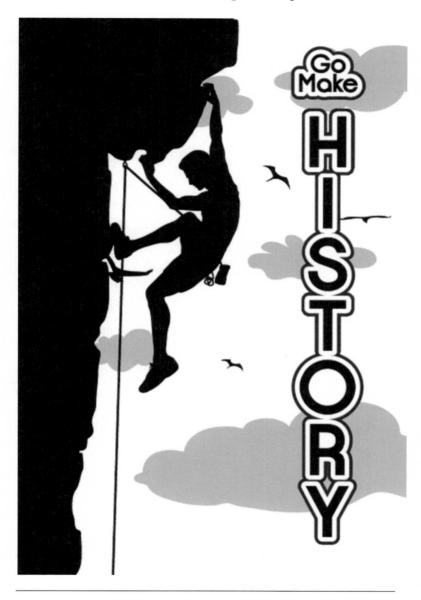

Law 19: Be Bold

THOSE WHO DO THE IMPOSSIBLE are famous for doing things that many would call crazy. They're called too risky, out of control, impulsive, or nuts. But the critics are often the people who didn't have the guts to make bold moves themselves, people who are now looking to justify their own unadventurous path. This is where the great ones separate themselves from the pack: What others call risky they see as pioneering.

If you take an inventory of your life, you will find out that we all are where we are due to a handful of major decisions we've made at certain stages of our lives. The day-to-day decisions are important as well, but our lives are charted by major decisions. Most of us can remember all of our life-changing moments. Here are some that I can think from my own life:

> 1. November 28, 1990: The day our family finally made it to America, a day I'll never forget.

2. March 27, 1997: I made the decision to join the US Army. That decision has influenced a big part of my life.

3. April 21, 2004: I made the decision to become a born-again Christian. I finally felt a huge burden lifted off of my back. I learned how to take support and guidance from a Higher Power.

4. June 26, 2009: My sweetheart and I got married. That was the fastest day of my life.

5. September 25, 2009: We decided to start People Helping People (PHP) with a group of courageous young leaders who wanted to make an impact on America, at a time that it was needed the most. PHP is a financial services company with a mission to help restore America by teaching basic financial fundamentals to the American people.

I probably have several other decisions that were important as well, but not ones that will dictate the rest of my life. Have you ever taken inventory of the biggest decisions you've made in your life? How did they turn out? Did you take the easy path or the tough one? Why do you think that is? It's not just about having the courage to make bold decisions, but also the dedication to stick with those decisions, win or lose.

"Nothing is more difficult, and therefore more precious, than to be able to decide."

— *Napoleon Bonaparte*

I'm a believer of running your big decisions by your mentors or trusted advisors. Your sounding board needs to be people who you respect and who have proven their ability to pioneer their own bold moves. Too many times I see people who have the capacity to do something really special in their lives take counsel from those who are afraid and indecisive.

We are not guaranteed tomorrow. People die every day in unexpected and sudden ways. Whether you meet your Maker tomorrow or fifty years from now, wouldn't you rather be on your death bed knowing that you gave it all you had instead of taking the easy path?

"You must be single minded. Drive for the one thing on which you have decided."

— *General George S. Patton, Jr.*

I challenge you to make the bold moves that you know deep down inside you need to make to do the impossible. There is of course no guarantee that everything will turn out the way that you plan, but what's more painful than living the rest of your life with the burden of what if?

Making bold moves is not about being reckless or impulsive (although some may call you that); it's about making your decisions wisely with trusted counsel and then taking the leap into uncharted territory. Odds are that some of your life-defining decisions have already been made. You can't change the past; but with boldness, you have the opportunity to shape your future.

Action Items

Write down five bold moves you're going to make in the next ninety days. The key is to be very specific.

1. _____

2. _____

3. _____

4. _____

5. _____

Recommended Videos

11 Skills that Millionaires Master:
http://www.patrickbetdavid.com/skills-millionaires-master/

How to Break Barriers:
https://www.youtube.com/watch?v=egL0pfUPoO4

Law 20: Embrace Your Frustrations

MANY OF THE PEOPLE WE'VE DISCUSSED in this book were extremely frustrated with an aspect of their lives at some point. Whether it was being frustrated financially, emotionally, spiritually, physically, or with an issue in their personal relationships, frustration challenged them to snap out of where they were and change. Whatever you don't hate, you will learn to tolerate. While many people don't like their jobs or their financial situation, those who do the impossible usually hate their current circumstances. They can't stand not having their vision become a reality. It eats at them until they figure out how to turn frustrations into fuel for their fire.

Frustration is a negative emotion, but it is often the source of a lot of positive changes. Think about how often frustration with the way things are leads to invention, innovation, and inspiration. Many great new ideas come out of frustration with the status quo. Frustration can be a great source of motivation.

"I've come to believe that all my past failure and frustrations were actually laying the foundation for the under- standings that have created the new level of thinking that I now enjoy."

— *Tony Robbins*

Losing weight is difficult for many people; but when someone gets frustrated enough with the way he looks, or the way his clothes fit, or the health effects of being overweight, that person does what it takes to drop the weight. Often times the frustration of not having enough money motivates someone to take the leap in his career or as an entrepreneur. Vision is imagining the future that you want to create, starting with the things that you want to change.

"Change will come ONLY when the pain of staying the same is greater than the pain of change."

— *Dora Lee Scott*

Everyone will become frustrated by something at some point in life, probably many times. Many people will simply complain about their frustration or accept it as a fact of life. It is up to you to be the kind of person who uses your frustration as inspiration to change your circumstances. Those who do the impossible conquer their frustration, not the other way around.

Action Items

1. List current situations that frustrate you.

2. Score them from one to ten on the level of importance.

3. What's the solution in order to change the situation?

Frustration:	Score:
Solution: _____	
_____	
_____	

Frustration:	Score:
Solution: _____	
_____	
_____	

Frustration:	Score:
Solution: _____	
_____	
_____	

Recommended Video

Why We Lose Momentum and How to Regain It:

http://www.patrickbetdavid.com/why-we-lose-momentum-how-to-regain-it/

Law 21: Fight Adversity Like Muhammad Ali

I FIRST LEARNED ABOUT TOUGHNESS from my dad. I remember being a child in Iran during the Iran-Iraq War. We lived in fear of the sound of alarms that warned of impending bombs. Those were some of the toughest years in the lives of the Bet-David family. My mom was the one who would bundle us up under the stairs when the alarms went off. But my dad was like a general in war: His face and his voice let us know that he wouldn't let anything happen to us. He told us every- thing would be alright, and we believed him, because he was the toughest man we knew.

I remember heading for a safer city (in our stylish white two-door Renault) as the bombs dropped behind us in Tehran. On the way, we were crossing a bridge and we heard a huge boom behind us. Like any father, my dad told us to not look back. Like any children, we looked back anyway and saw that a huge bomb had dropped fifty yards behind us and left nothing but rubble it its wake. To this day, my sister and I talk about how we can hear that awful explosion and see the destruction just yards behind us as if it had happened yesterday.

I think that day was the end of it for my mom, the day she decided that we had to get out of Iran and come to America. The toughness and resilience that my parents had to have to get their family from war-torn Iran to the United States is something that gave me personal insight into toughness. My parents' toughness is the reason that I am here today, in America, writing a book on doing the impossible. They showed us how to do the impossible in our own lives by setting the example and doing the impossible for our family.

> *"For a tree to become tall it must grow tough roots among the rocks."*
>
> — *Friedrich Nietzsche*

Sports give us great examples of toughness and playing while hurt. Think about Kirk Gibson hitting the winning home run in the 1988 World Series and limping around the bases with his injured leg. Remember Curt Shilling with his famous bloody sock beating the New York Yankees in the 2004 quest for the pennant?

How many boxers have won their bout with one eye swollen shut and a cracked rib?

When it comes to sports, business, leadership, and life, the great ones are tough: They learn to play while hurt. Being tough means playing through physical pain, emotional stress, and all the difficulties that life drops on us from time to time. It also means playing through the doubts of others and the harsh words of critics.

All of us play while hurt at some point in our lives. It's not playing while hurt itself that separates us from the rest; it's how we choose to play while hurt. It's how you do what needs to be done even on the days that you don't feel well, how you put a smile on your face and lead the meeting when you just got stressful news from home. Successfully playing while hurt means giving 100% on days when you only feel 50%.

> *"I hated every minute of training, but I said, 'Don't quit.*
> *Suffer now and live the rest of your life as a champion.'"*
>
> — *Muhammad Ali*

How is toughness developed? Is it a God given talent or something that we acquire? Toughness is normally developed through events that create a high level of pressure. The way you respond to those events will determine your level of toughness. I believe it is God challenging us to see how badly we want to do the impossible in life. You have to believe that you will reap the reward for making it through all twelve rounds, especially during those times when all you want to do is throw in the towel. Achieving great things takes dedication on the good days and the bad days.

The list of people who had to develop the toughness of a fighter in order for them to do the impossible is long. Many times they were taken advantage of, lost a loved one, went bankrupt, or fought through physical or health challenges. For some, it seemed all odds were against them until they did the impossible. That's why it's very important for us to be grateful for the challenges we've gone through in our lives: They are building blocks for doing the impossible. Perseverance in challenging situations actually develops you into the person who you will need to be in order to accomplish the impossible. Those trials are the fire that heats us up so we can be molded into a new person. If you let your difficulties and hurts in life shape you by toughing it out, you'll come out transformed on the other side.

Action Items

Make a list of people in your life who you would consider tough and why. (Not celebrities, but friends, family, or acquaintances.)

Name	Why

Recommended Videos

Muhammad Ali- 10 Things Entrepreneurs Can Learn From Him:

http://www.patrickbetdavid.com/muhammad-ali-10-things-entrepreneurs-can-learn/

Law 22: Let Controversy Be Your Status Quo

MOST PEOPLE THINK that being controversial is some- thing negative, but that's not always the case. Controversy is a part of life. "Controversial" is often a description for words or decisions that will make a person less liked. How often do parents have to make decisions with their kids that are not the most popular? Anyone with a teenager knows what it's like to get the silent treatment after a parenting decision that your teen found "controversial."

These are some basic decisions that we make that could possibly be looked at as controversial by someone:

1. Leaving your job to start a business.

2. Having to put up with hearing comments such as "I hate you" from your sixteen-year-old daughter for not allowing her to go on a date with a twenty-year-old.

3. Talking about politics or religion with some of your coworkers.

4. Dropping out of college to start a business.

5. Stepping away from your family-owned business to create your own identity.

6. Leaving the city you grew up in to pursue your life-long dreams in another place.

7. Doing the total opposite of what everybody else does.

Most people want to be extremely careful to say all the right things and do everything "by the book." The world has taught us that if we play it safe and just follow the system, everything will work out. Those who do the impossible do the total opposite.

It's a very normal thing for those who do the impossible to rub people the wrong way at times. They always have an enemy or a competitor who would like to see them gone. The best way to never have others dislike you is to never do anything worth noticing.

> *"Confidence comes not from always being right but from not fearing to be wrong."*
>
> — *Peter T. McIntyre*

We have created this image in our minds of Jesus being a nice man who loved everyone and wanted everyone to be happy. Jesus did love everyone, but He wasn't loved by everyone in return. If you read the Bible, you'll find out that Jesus rubbed many people the wrong way. He wasn't afraid to challenge conventional thinking and the religious elites of the time. You better believe that Jesus made enemies. Declaring He was the Son of God was definitely controversial.

> *"A successful man is one who can lay a firm foundation with the bricks others have thrown at him."*
>
> — *David Brinkley*

Recently I was reading The 100: A Ranking of the Most Influential Persons in History by Michael H. Heart. What I noticed right away was that most of the people on the list were controversial in their time. They were so certain about their set of beliefs that they were willing to fight for it until the end. They didn't understand the concept of status quo. Nowhere in history will you find someone who either changed the world or challenged the thinking of a nation by just going with the flow.

> *"The reasonable man adapts himself to the world; the unreasonable one persists in trying to adapt the world to himself. Therefore all progress depends on the unreasonable man."*
>
> — *George Bernard Shaw*

Here are some of the names from Heart's list that you might recognize:

- Muhammad
- Sir Isaac Newton
- Jesus Christ
- Confucius
- Saint Paul
- Christopher Columbus
- Albert Einstein
- Galileo
- John Locke
- Henry Ford
- Homer
- Alexander the Great
- Genghis Kahn
- Thomas Edison
- Sigmund Freud
- Nicoli Machiavelli
- Charlemagne
- Adam Smith

- Julius Cesar

- George Washington

One of the qualities that we've all been given by our Creator is the desire to be liked. Some claim that they don't care what people think of them, but everyone cares to some extent. Human beings seek out love, approval, and respect from their spouse, family, friends, and coworkers every day.

Still, as much as we love harmony, people also love controversy. We respect those who are brave enough to be different and strong enough to stand with the courage of their convictions. Many people from history who are considered heroes today were the heretics of their time.

Doing the impossible means challenging the normal way of thinking, going against the grain, and carving out a new path that other people can't yet see.

Action Items

#1: Do you catch yourself trying to please everyone? If so, why? _____

#2: How do you feel when people talk about you behind your back?

_____

#3: Do you typically avoid conflicts? Yes or no. If yes, why?

_____

#4: What are three things you can do right away in order to improve in the area of dealing with conflicts?

1. _____

2. _____

3._____

Recommended Videos

How to Handle the Highs and Lows of Life:

http://www.patrickbetdavid.com/highs-and-lows-of-life/

How to Respond When You Don't Hit a Goal:

http://www.patrickbetdavid.com/respond-to-loss-as-an-entrepreneur/

12 Mistakes I Made my First Year as an Entrepreneur:

http://www.patrickbetdavid.com/mistakes-made-first-year-entrepreneur/

Law 23: Silence Your Critics

THIS COULD BE A CONTROVERSIAL CHAPTER for some of you because many of us have been taught by our parents, teachers, and pastors not to be motivated by proving people wrong. That's good advice if you are a twelve- year-old kid and a seventeen-year-old tells you that you're not tough enough to smoke a cigarette and you prove him wrong by smoking it. But there are many times in life when the drive to prove our critics wrong can actually push us to better ourselves.

For example:

• The person who loses twenty pounds because he gets invited to a wedding that his ex is attending.

• The kid who is bullied by someone older or bigger, which inspires him to learn how to defend himself and show the bully that he's not easy pickings. (Wanderlei Silva, Forrest Griffen, Kevin Randleman, and Andrei Arlovski are all UFC Fighters who say they were bullied when they were young.)

• The teenager who is told he must ride the bench, which he uses as motivation to practice more, get better, and come back as first string. (Many of the guys who are in the big leagues today are there because a coach doubted them at one point. Michael Jordan was actually cut from his high school basketball team!)

In life, we all have people who doubt us and tell us what we can't do. The bigger the goal that you set, the more you will hear "it can't be done." Impossibility thinkers turn that criticism into motivation. They are compelled by a need to silence their critics. The words "it can't be done" to them sound like "prove me wrong."

Have you ever had a teacher, a friend, or a relative give you a look of doubt when you tell them what you plan to accomplish? Has anyone ever told you that your goals are unrealistic? If not, you might need to set your sights higher; being doubted is a mile maker on the road to greatness.

When you set out to do the impossible, you will be faced with doubt and rejection. What separates the great ones from the pack is the way that they react to that criticism. To most people, negative feedback can be discouraging; but a few are able to actually turn it into fuel for their fire.

History is packed with a long list of examples of great achievers whose detractors predicted they would fail:

•George Steinbrenner didn't start off being the successful owner of the Yankees. He first owned the Cleveland Pipers. Never heard of them? The franchise eventually went bankrupt and Steinbrenner, $125,000 in debt with personal losses of $2 million, eventually silenced his critics by turning the New York Yankees into one of the most valuable franchises in sports history.

• Harry Potter author, J.K. Rowling was rejected by twelve different publishers when she first wrote the book. Several publishers even told her to "get a real job." Now she's the second richest female entertainer after Oprah.

• Most think of Einstein's name as synonymous with genius, but he didn't always come across that way. Einstein didn't speak until he was four and did not read until he was seven. His teachers and parents thought he was mentally handicapped, slow, and anti-social. Eventually, he was expelled from school and was refused admittance to the Zurich Polytechnic School. But years later,no one was calling Einstein "slow" when he was winning the Nobel Prize for his breakthroughs in physics.

• After his first audition, Sidney Poitier was told by the casting director, "Why don't you stop wasting people's time and go out and become a dish- washer or something?" Poitier vowed to show him that he could make it, going on to win an Oscar and becoming one of the most respected actors of all time.

• In his first film, Harrison Ford was told by the movie execs that he simply didn't have what it takes to be a star. Today, with dozens of hit movies playing iconic characters like Indiana Jones and Han Solo, Ford can proudly show that he does in fact have what it takes.

• We know Elvis Presley as one of the best-selling artists of all time. But back in 1954, Elvis was a nobody. The manager of the Grand Ole Opry fired Elvis after just one performance, telling him, "You ain't goin' nowhere, son. You ought to go back to drivin' a truck."

Of all the examples of great ones silencing their critics, the first person who comes to my mind is always Muhammad Ali. I was fortunate enough to be able to visit The Muhammad Ali Center in Kentucky. I learned that there was a time when everyone around Ali doubted him—media, friends, and even family.

Ali didn't just ignore the criticism of others; instead he used it as motivation. His dream became not just to be a champion, but to prove all the people who doubted him wrong. There is no better way to silence your critics than to make them eat their words. But always be grateful for your critics and use their doubt as fuel in your tank for doing the impossible.

> *"Criticism is something you can avoid easily—by saying nothing, doing nothing, and being nothing."*
>
> *— Aristotle*

Action Items

#1: Who has ever doubted you? How did you react to their doubt? What kind of power do they have over you?

Nam	Reaction	Powe

#2: What can you do differently the next time someone doubts your capacity to do the impossible?

_____

_____

_____

Law 24: Charge Your Batteries with Challenges

THERE WAS A TIME IN MY LIFE when I was one of the laziest people you could ever meet. All I wanted to do was watch sports and play video games. I had a 1.8 GPA in high school and I didn't apply myself at anything. I definitely wasn't challenging myself. Later in life, I became curious as to why some people are lazy and others are driven in life. I discovered that laziness stems from boredom—from not being challenged or not pursuing a goal. We are lazy when we're not growing and not being forced to elevate our thinking.

Have you ever watched a boring movie? What happens? You all of a sudden start feeling sleepy.

That's because you're bored. Likewise, when we are chronically tired, it is often because we are uninterested in life. If life is making you tired, ask yourself, what are you on the hunt for? What has captured your imagination?

When no real challenge faces us, we get mentally and physically lethargic. Napoleon Bonaparte was known for his boundless energy and strength. He never let himself rest and he was never satisfied with what he had achieved. Napoleon once said, "Sometimes death only comes from a lack of energy." A lack of energy comes from not being challenged, when we have taken on less than we are capable of. Have you taken on as much as you are capable of? Are you taking the easy route or pushing yourself? Or have you maxed out your life? Are you happy or simply con- tent? Contentment can be found living life on cruise control. But happiness comes from being challenged, growing as a person, and chasing a dream.

> *"Without passion you don't have energy, without energy you have nothing."*
>
> — *Donald Trump*

We spend about a third of our waking hours working. That's a lot of hours of boredom if your job doesn't inspire you. Have you ever dreaded going to work in the morning and clocking in? Have you ever had a job where the later it got on Sunday night, the crankier you got because you hated going to your job the next day? We have all had to work uninspiring jobs at some point in our lives. In my experience, I was bored when I worked for a company that had no vision beyond making money.

Those who do the impossible don't consider their job to be work. I was asked once why we have to work so hard to achieve greatness. My answer was simple: I stopped working a long time ago. Now I live. I no longer consider my day filled with "work"; rather it is just part of life, and something that I look forward to every day. Most people are discouraged when you tell them that an eighty-hour work week is a formula for success. We all have 168 hours per week, but most people mentally separate their working hours (usually from nine to five) as a distinct part of their life. They often view work as a necessary evil. The key is to have no distinction between living and working. When your job is your passion, giving a speech, making phone calls, planning a strategy, or writing a business plan is not work; it's just another part of living. When you live your passion, you don't have to worry about energy or boredom. Chasing your dreams is the only caffeine that you will need.

> *"The more you lose yourself in something bigger than your- self, the more energy you will have."*
>
> *— Norman Vincent Peale*

Recommended Videos:

How to Handle Chaos as an Entrepreneur:

http://www.patrickbetdavid.com/how-to-handle-chaos-as-an-entrepreneur/

Why Underdogs Make the Best Entrepreneurs:

http://www.patrickbetdavid.com/underdogs-make-best-entrepreneurs/

The 2 Challenges Every Entrepreneur Will Face:

http://www.patrickbetdavid.com/challenges-every-entrepreneur-will-face/

10 Things to be Paranoid About as an Entrepreneur:

http://www.patrickbetdavid.com/paranoid-about-as-an-entrepreneur/

Law 25: Have Heart

ACCORDING TO THE DICTIONARY, courage is the "mental or moral strength to venture, persevere, and withstand danger, fear, or difficulty."

You have to have courage if you want to do something special in your life. Courage is a common thread among all the great ones.

Years ago, Latin was considered a must-learn language in many schools. Today Latin is a rarely taught or used language. But the Latin roots of many English words have left us with a treasured vocabulary. Looking at the Latin roots of our words gives us insight into their meaning. Courage comes from the Latin corāticum, meaning heart. Heart is the core of courage because it is the source from which the characteristics of courage emanate.

Think about what we mean when we say:

That fighter has heart!

That player has heart!

That soldier has heart!

What we are really saying is that person has courage.

I want to share some quotes with you about courage that do a better job than I could at explaining why courage is so important:

> *"Without courage, all other virtues lose their meaning." —Sir Winston Churchill*
>
> *"Courage is not simply one of the virtues but the form of every virtue at the testing point." —C.S. Lewis*
>
> *"Wealth lost—something lost; honor lost— much lost; courage lost—all lost." —Old German Proverb*
>
> *"In times of stress be bold and valiant." —Horace*
>
> *"Fortune and love favor the brave." —Ovid*
>
> *"True miracles are created by men when they use the courage and intelligence that God gave them." —Jean Anouilh*

Courage is the virtue with which every other virtue is reinforced when tested. Throughout history, courage has been at the heart of every impossible achievement.

When you think of the great ones throughout history, what is the one thing that they all had in common? They had to have courage. Martin Luther King had to have a ton of courage to stand up for equal rights in the 1960s. Billy Graham had the courage to take God's Message into totalitarian dictatorships like Communist

Russia, Eastern Europe, and North Korea. Ronald Reagan had to have courage to call the Soviet Union an "Evil Empire" and to demand that Gorbachev "tear down this wall." Alexander the Great could not have conquered two million square miles of the planet without immense courage.

> *"The journey of a thousand miles starts with a single step."*
>
> — *Chinese Proverb*

We look up to those people who have the courage to venture into the unknown and persevere. We admire leaders and visionaries, people who have the courage to do what most people don't think is possible. It's the feeling that we have when we watch movies like Braveheart, Lean on Me, 300, Men of Honor, and Rocky. Human beings admire people of courage. We make movies about them so that we can feel like a part of their story, even just for a couple of hours. But we can do more than look up to the courageous in history and the movies: We can emulate them. So the question is: Do some have more courage than others? The answer is yes. Just like we strengthen the muscles in our body by putting them to use, you can strengthen your "courage muscle" by putting yourself into situations that require courage.

The more you use the courage you already have, the more you develop your courage.

Here are some examples of things that take courage in everyday life:

• Talking to the girl who you really liked in high school when you were afraid she might reject you

• Asking the love of your life to marry you

• Deciding to have kids

• Becoming a first-time entrepreneur

• Leaving your job to start a small business

•Moving your family from another country to America

• Sharing your faith with someone

• Sharing your opinion about politics with a group

• Deciding to write a book when English was your worst subject in school

• Reading this book and implementing the principles

People have come up to me and said, "But Patrick, I don't have courage like you do." The above list should show you that you have more courage than you think. In order for you to take it to the next level, you need to put yourself in situations that take you out of your comfort zone. Courage is a gift from God. It is there inside for us to access, but we have to actively reach for it. Courage is a must for those who want to do   the impossible.

"A ship in a harbor is safe, but that's not what ships are built for."

— Unknown

Recommended Videos
A Message from 75-Year-Old You:
https://www.youtube.com/watch?v=ieF78rjNLyE

10 Unmeasurable Qualities of a Human Being:
http://www.patrickbetdavid.com/unmeasurable-qualities-human-beings/

The Life of an Entrepreneur in 90 Seconds:
http://www.patrickbetdavid.com/life-entrepreneur-90-seconds/

Final Challenge

MY FINAL CHALLENGE TO YOU as you finish this book is to have a blast throughout the entire journey of doing the impossible. Over the years I've had the privilege of working with many different personalities, and it's always interesting to see how different people approach doing the impossible. I've seen people who are miserable in their journey, and I've seen others who have fun throughout the entire process. While enjoying the ride may not be necessary to being successful, if you're not having a blast, you are missing the point.

The best way to look at the journey of doing the impossible is to look at your life like an Academy Award- winning movie with an incredible ending. A great film keeps you excited because you don't know what will happen next. If you look at life as an adventure, you will learn to enjoy the ups, downs, and twists along the way.

There will be days where you just may question your capacity to finish what you started, but keep in mind that you're a lot closer than you think you are. Embrace the times where you have no clue what to do next. Learn to anticipate the negative thoughts and questions that come during late nights at the office alone:

What was I thinking?

What if they are right and I don't have what it takes to do this?

Why am I putting myself through this?

Why am I even reading a book called Doing the Impossible?

Is it really worth it?

While all of this is going through your mind, remind yourself what life could look like if you achieve what you've set out to do. Think of the memories you'll share with your loved ones for the rest of your life and the level of confidence you'll have from proving to yourself that you are a person who finishes what you start. Think about the look on your parents' faces and how proud they are of you for fighting through the tough times and not giving up.

You can't put a price tag on any of that. None of these experiences and emotions can be purchased at the mall or ordered on the internet. They can only be earned. It's a feeling that no drug or drink could EVER replace. And as good as you think it's going to feel, I'm here to tell you that it is one hundred times better than you ever imagined.

I remember the year 2001 as the lowest point of my life. I was in a relationship that wasn't going anywhere. I was at a terrible place financially; I was twenty-two years old with twenty-six credit cards and $49,000 of debt. I crammed my 6'5" frame into an old Ford Focus every day, because that's all I could afford. My father had several heart attacks during this period and I was certain I was going to lose him. I felt like all the odds were stacked against me and there wasn't anything that I could do right. I was about ready to give up and resign myself to a life of mediocrity. But something inside of me kept saying that I was meant to do something special with my life

It wasn't as simple as making a decision to change my life; I still had to do the hard work. I was forced to go back and get a job working at a gym where I once was a manager. Since minimum wage wasn't cutting it, I started selling t-shirts on the corner to earn a few extra bucks. I would wake up early in the morning to go to downtown LA and buy shirts for $2.00 and sell them for $10.00. Friends who I went to school with would see me selling shirts on the side of the street and ask me what I was doing. My ego took a huge beating. But all I knew was that I didn't like the direction my life had been taking and only I could change my course. My family deserved a better life and I felt that I had to step up and deliver for them.

My parents sacrificed a lot to bring us to America. Growing up, we were never wealthy. I remember at six years old asking my dad what heaven looked like. He told me that there's an Island next to California called Hawaii and that it's the closest thing to heaven. My dad said one day he'd take me there. Unfortunately, due to his health (thirteen heart attacks, six angiograms, six angioplasties, and three stents in his heart), he wasn't ever able to take us to Hawaii. As an adult, I became driven by a burning desire to take my dad to Hawaii and experience "heaven" with him. It became a driving force for me to develop a lifestyle with the resources to make those dreams come true, for me and my family. My dad and I have now been to Hawaii together seven times.

In the last ten years we've been able to experience things that we never thought were possible. Many of these kinds of experiences cost money; but you can't put a price tag on them, because money has nothing to do with the value of experiences. As we lie on our death beds, I highly doubt we'll be thinking about the expensive cars, nice homes, or jewelry we've had; but I'm certain we'll be thinking about the moments and experiences that gave our lives meaning.

The point of this chapter is to encourage you and challenge you to have fun throughout the entire process.

Learn to enjoy the fun times as well as the times where you feel like giving up. Both kinds of experiences are what makes your journey that much more meaningful. Our lives are really a highlight reel of all of our most moving experiences. That is what we will remember at the end. These are the moments that make us who we are. So why not have as many of those kinds of experiences as possible? Why not explore the world? Why not experience what it feels like to do the impossible?

The journey of doing the impossible will be at times frustrating and fulfilling, at times exasperating and enjoyable; but it will always be worthwhile.

Action Items

#1:Make a list of experiences that you will forever cherish.

1. _____

2. _____

3. _____

4. _____

5. _____

#2: Make a list of new things or places you want to experience that you haven't yet.

1. _____

2. _____

3. _____

4. _____

5. _____

#3: Write down your life of the impossible. What are some things that you would like to do that may seem impossible at this time? Score them based on difficulty from one to ten. Note as well which one is the most important to you. Choose the one that's the most important to you at this stage of your life and from there, start your journey of doing the impossible.

Impossible : _____ Score:

_____

Note : _____

Impossible : _____ Score:

_____

Note : _____

Impossible : _____ Score:

_____

Note : _____

Endnotes

Law 1 - Invest in Your Identity

(1)http://en.wikipedia.org/wiki/Jack_Whittaker_(lott
ery_winner)

Law 7 - Work Like It's 1880

(2) Source: Fogel, Robert. The Fourth Great Awakening
and the Future of Egalitarianism. Chicago: University
of Chicago Press, 2000 Notes: Discretionary hours
exclude hours used for sleep, meals, and hygiene.
Work hours include paid work, travel to and from
work, and household chores.

Law 7 - Work Like It's 1880

(3)
        http://www.bls.gov/news.release/atus.nr0.ht
m Law 15 - Channel Your Obsession

(4)
http://www.psychologytoday.com/blog/entrepreneur

sadhd/200909/7-habits-highly-successful-
entrepreneurs-adhd

About the Author

Patrick's amazing story starts with his family immigrating to America when he was 10-years old. His parents fled Iran as refugees during the Iranian revolution and were eventually granted U.S. citizenship.

After high school Patrick joined the U.S. military and served in the 101st Airborne before starting a business career in the financial services industry. After a tenure with a couple of traditional companies, he was inspired to launch PHP Agency Inc., an insurance sales, marketing and distribution company – and did so before he turned 30. PHP is now one of the fastest growing companies in the financial marketplace.

Patrick is passionate about shaping the next generation of leaders by teaching thought-provoking perspectives on entrepreneurship and disrupting the traditional approach to a career. Patrick's popularity surged and created a buzz in the hearts of entrepreneurs all over the world when The Life of an Entrepreneur in 90 Seconds, a video he created, accumulated over 30 million views online (It became a book in June 2016: The Life of an Entrepreneur in 90 Pages). That video and scores of other videos comprise his library of edifying, educational and inspirational content about entrepreneurship – all available at Valuetainment, a media brand he conceived and founded.

Valuetainment exists to teach about the fundamentals of entrepreneurship and personal development while inspiring people to break from limiting beliefs or other constraints and achieve their dreams. It has been referred to as "the best channel for entrepreneurs."

Patrick speaks on a range of business, leadership and entrepreneurial topics including how and why to become an entrepreneur and the importance of learning how to fully process issues. He is particularly passionate about the need for every individual to pursue their desires, once stating, "Most of the greatest world changers and heroes of all time are at the graveyard undiscovered because they never sold out to their dreams and desires."

Patrick has also hosted a series of one-on-one interviews with some of the world's most interesting people, including NBA Hall of Famers James Worthy and Magic Johnson, Author Robert Greene, Billionaire Entrepreneur and NBA team owner Mark Cuban, Indy-500 Winner Al Unser Jr., Apple co-founder, Steve Wozniak, author and entrepreneur Robert Kiyosaki, and many others.

From a humble beginning as a young immigrant escaping war-torn Iran with his parents, to founding his own company, Patrick has gained a first-hand understanding of what rags-to-riches means and how it is fueled by freedom and opportunity – the core tenants of the American Dream.

Patrick resides in Dallas TX with his wife and three children. You explore Patrick's books and library of Valuetainment content at : www.patrickbetdavid.com

Other Books by Patrick Bet-David

The Life of An Entrepreneur in 90 Pages
http://www.patrickbetdavid.com/90-pages

The Next Perfect Storm:
http://www.patrickbetdavid.com/perfect-storm

More books coming soon. To see all books by Patrick Bet-David, visit his Amazon Author Page:

http://patrickbetdavid.com/amazon.

Made in the USA
Thornton, CO
07/21/22 16:17:34

08c32e3d-bad6-45af-abd1-589c4296c37bR01